LIFE WORLD LIBRARY

SWITZERLAND

OTHER BOOKS BY THE EDITORS OF LIFE

LIFE Nature Library

LIFE Science Library

The LIFE History of the United States

LIFE Pictorial Atlas of the World

The Epic of Man

The Wonders of Life on Earth

The World We Live In

The World's Great Religions

The LIFE Book of Christmas

LIFE's Picture History of Western Man

The LIFE Treasury of American Folklore

America's Arts and Skills

The Second World War

LIFE's Picture History of World War II

Picture Cook Book

LIFE Guide to Paris

LIFE WORLD LIBRARY

SWITZERLAND

by Herbert Kubly

and The Editors of LIFE

A STONEHENGE BOOK

TIME INCORPORATED   NEW YORK

COVER: A balloonist makes last-minute
preparations for ascent at the Second
International Ballooning Week in Mürren.
After rising from the ground, he will float
over the Alps to Turin, Italy.

ABOUT THE WRITER

Herbert Kubly, the author of the interpretive text for this volume, is an
American of Swiss ancestry, having been born and brought up in New
Glarus, Wisconsin, a farming community made up of descendants of im-
migrants to the United States from the canton of Glarus in Switzerland.
A lifelong student of things Swiss, Mr. Kubly, who has traveled through
Switzerland several times, revisited the country immediately before writing
this volume to refresh his memory and to interview a number of Switzer-
land's most influential present-day businessmen and thinkers.

A graduate of the University of Wisconsin, Mr. Kubly is known to
American readers as the author of *American in Italy*, which won the National Book Award in 1956. In addition he has written another travel
book, *Easter in Sicily;* a volume of short stories, *Varieties of Love;* a novel,
The Whistling Zone; and a recent volume of essays, *At Large*. He is the
author of the interpretive text for the LIFE World Library volume on Italy.
He has been a newspaper reporter, an art and music critic, and an associate professor of speech at the University of Illinois. He currently teaches
English at the New School for Social Research in New York City.

During his most recent trip to Switzerland, Mr. Kubly traveled to his
ancestral village of Elm in Glarus. There, on a visit to a high summer
pasture on the Mühlebach alp above Elm, he chanced to meet and stay
with a distant relative, Jakob Kubli, and his sons. The refreshing story of
this encounter may be found in Chapter 8 of this volume.

Switzerland © 1964 by Time Inc. All rights reserved. Published simultaneously in Canada.
Library of Congress catalogue card number 64-17697.
School and library distribution by Silver Burdett Company.

Contents

TIME-LIFE BOOKS

EDITOR
Norman P. Ross
TEXT DIRECTOR   ART DIRECTOR
William Jay Gold   Edward A. Hamilton
CHIEF OF RESEARCH
Beatrice T. Dobie
Assistant Text Director: Jerry Korn
Assistant Chief of Research: Monica O. Horne

•

PUBLISHER
Rhett Austell
General Manager: John A. Watters
Business Manager: John D. McSweeney
Circulation Manager: Joan D. Lanning

LIFE MAGAZINE

EDITOR: Edward K. Thompson
MANAGING EDITOR: George P. Hunt
PUBLISHER: Jerome S. Hardy

LIFE WORLD LIBRARY
Editorial Staff for *Switzerland:*
EDITOR: Oliver E. Allen
Assistant to the Editor: David S. Thomson
Designer: Ben Schultz
Chief Researcher: Grace Brynolson
Researchers: Madeleine Bittel Richards, Jill Adams, Sondra Albert,
Barbara Ballantine, Sue Bond, Edward Brash, Evelyn Hauptman
Picture Researchers: Margaret K. Goldsmith, Barbara Sullivan
Art Associate: Robert L. Young
Art Assistants: James D. Smith, James K. Davis
Copy Staff: Marian Gordon Goldman, Helen Isaacs, Dolores A. Littles

The interpretive text for the chapters of this book was written by Herbert Kubly and the picture essays were written by Edmund V. White and David S. Thomson. Many of the photographs were taken by Farrell Grehan. Valuable help was provided by the following individuals and departments of Time Inc.: Doris O'Neil, Chief of the LIFE Picture Library; Content Peckham, Chief of the Bureau of Editorial Reference; and Richard M. Clurman, Chief of the TIME-LIFE News Service.

Introduction

Victor Hugo wrote that in history Switzerland will have the last word. In the light of current history, this statement is hard to refute. Certainly no other nation today can equal the Swiss achievement of finding advantage in adversity, of maintaining unity in a diverse and varied society, and of adapting to the complexities of modern life while clinging tenaciously to historic values and traditions.

In this volume, Herbert Kubly has traced the historical forces and the various contributions from many cultures which have gone into the formation of a society uniquely Swiss. Some of his observations may be controversial, but he has done valuable service in delving beneath the traditional image of Switzerland to portray the complex forces constantly at work in this dynamic and progressive nation. He points out the many paradoxes which have been resolved to create modern Switzerland without abandoning the country's original philosophy. A technologically advanced industrial system exists side by side with a pastoral agriculture. A complete welfare program has been established within a political framework founded in the Middle Ages. Perhaps most remarkable has been Switzerland's ability to mediate between other nations without either becoming involved itself or giving up any of its national sovereignty or identity. Switzerland has actively contributed toward European and worldwide consolidation, and has exercised a moral influence far beyond its actual power while steadfastly defending the neutrality which is the cornerstone of its foreign policy.

Their history has forced upon the Swiss those qualities which today enable them to play this international role. To stay united and strong in a Europe shaken by the national and religious schisms of the post-Renaissance era, the Swiss had perforce to learn tolerance, to find peaceful solutions to international problems and to practice the industry and frugality which characterize their economic life. Their neutral policy was adopted to keep their tiny country from being sundered by the giants surrounding it. But it has not been a static policy. Mr. Kubly speculates on the modern role of Swiss neutrality at a time when Europe is increasingly united and the world increasingly divided between capitalist and Communist, industrial and agrarian economies, and white and non-white peoples. The adjustment will be difficult, particularly as Switzerland is so clearly capitalist, industrial and white. But it is safe to say that whatever develops will be in the spirit of that blend of pragmatism and idealism that the Swiss have made so particularly their own.

The Swiss state and the Swiss people merit careful study by old and new nations alike. To this study LIFE World Library has provided an attractive and rewarding introduction.

C. BURKE ELBRICK
former Assistant Secretary of State
for European Affairs

1

The Everlasting League

AN American arriving not long ago in the square in front of the Parliament building in Bern found it filled not with official cars, uniformed guards and bustling bureaucrats but with flowers and vegetables. Apple-cheeked country women in embroidered costumes, their stalls cornucopias of produce which seem to grow larger in Switzerland than in the rest of the world, were selling cucumbers 20 inches long, radishes like apples and cabbages harder and larger than soccer balls.

Leaving the noise and crush of the market, the visitor entered the Germanic Renaissance-style Parliament building and found himself standing in a great hall among huge vases of delphinium and a pair of bronze bears, the animal symbols of Bern. He heard a footstep and turned to face a moustached, short-legged man in a baggy Chaplinesque uniform with a medallion indicating he was a guide.

Recognizing the visitor as an American, the guide explained that the building was not only the capitol of Switzerland but was also "the White House," containing the executive offices of the federal government.

The American asked the name of the president and the guide looked at him with startled eyes. "Let's see, who is president?" he said, mumbling and scratching his head. Suddenly he darted out through a door. In a moment he reappeared, and with triumph in his voice announced, "It's Herr Spühler. Willy Spühler is President now!"

For an American, whose governmental system makes the president such a pivotal and powerful figure, it was a curious lesson in democracy. Switzerland changes presidents every year, and many citizens never bother to remember the name of the present incumbent. The Swiss have a taste for anonymity and mistrust people who rise too far above the herd. Heredity and wealth are political detriments for a Swiss. The president, who rents his modest apartment and pays the salary of his single maid himself, is expected to ride to work on the streetcar.

FOR the truth is that while Switzerland sometimes seems to resemble those miniature mythological republics that were the scenes of old-fashioned comic operas, it is really the most practical, the most hardheaded, the most enduring democracy in the world. It is also one of the most contradictory. Here are a few of Switzerland's contradictions:

It is a federation of 25 sovereign states, called cantons, with a people drawn from three ethnic, two religious and four linguistic groups, but these people have maintained themselves as a nation for more than six centuries.

In its natural resources the poorest country in Europe, Switzerland is, by per capita income, one of the richest countries in the world.

Although the Swiss are happy to let the rest of the world think that their country is still an Alpine Arcadia of gamboling goats and jolly peasants, Switzerland is intensely industrialized and, next to England and Belgium, has a smaller proportion of its people engaged in agriculture than any other country in Europe.

The people of Switzerland squabbled among themselves and with their neighbors until a century ago, and were famous for their belligerence. Since then, while the world around them has been periodically collapsing into chaos, they have lived in uninterrupted peace.

A traditionally conservative people with a professed fear of all Left-Wing political philosophies, the Swiss live under a highly developed system of welfare paternalism.

A country which prides itself on its social advances, Switzerland is one of the few countries in the world in which women are not permitted to vote in national elections.

How, amid such contradictions, did the homogeneity of Switzerland come about? For the answer one must look to the mountains, and to the type of men—solitary, independent and frugal—which mountains breed.

A balloonist who sometimes floats visitors over the Alps at a spot near the 13,648-foot-high Jungfrau can, on a clear day, indicate with a sweep of his arm the whole of Switzerland. One sees an inland island roughly the size of Massachusetts and New Hampshire combined, much of it a plain contained by two mountain systems and a river. The Jura range begins in the west and curves northeastward, forming a frontier between Switzerland and France. The Alps dominate the southern part of the country, making a natural frontier between Switzerland and Italy. The Rhine forms the country's northern border with Germany and part of its eastern border with Austria.

THE balloonist can look out on a diminishing horizon of snow-covered peaks, which rise from a thousand dark valleys like a sea of whitecaps. Below and to the east are the Bernese Oberland and the Gotthard massif, the central segment of the Alps. The glaciers over which the balloon drifts are the apex of the European watershed, from which waters flow to all corners of Europe and to the seas surrounding it by way of the Inn and the Danube to the Black Sea, by the Ticino and Po Rivers to the Adriatic, and within a few miles of one another, cascading apart at their very sources, by the Rhine flowing toward the cold North Sea and the Rhone flowing toward the warm Mediterranean. If the balloon were to waft high enough, its passengers might be able to see Switzerland's three outposts overlooking foreign soil: Basel, facing Germany and France; Geneva, virtually surrounded by French territory; and Lugano, confronting Italy. It is easy to understand how such a natural redoubt was destined for an international role.

SWITZERLAND'S landscape is probably the most diverse and overwhelmingly beautiful in the world. In the single day that it takes to drive across the country in any direction, one passes through a dozen different types of scenery and half as many climates. The most dramatic entrance is in the south, from Italy, through the border town of Chiasso, past the silver-misted Lake of Lugano with its lush tropical shores of palms and the soporific scents of honeysuckle and jasmine. The land and light here are Mediterranean, with the profiles of mountains stark against the blue skies, and the stone houses, smothered by roses and wisteria, seemingly carved out of the rocks like caves.

The road up to the 7,101-foot-high St. Gotthard Pass is a serpent coiling in and about tiny hillside villages and terraced vineyards; the guidebook lists more than 30 hairpin curves. Trees change from chestnut to fir and then disappear altogether as one approaches the top of the pass. In the dark canyons torrents roar and the air is cold. After a three-hour drive one reaches the summit, a glacial tundra of white snow patches, brown lichen and pools of gray water. It is a relief to leave the bleak elemental landscape and descend into a green world where men and women are cutting hay and hanging it on racks to dry.

In crossing the St. Gotthard Pass we have traveled from a wine to a milk culture. The small hillside meadows are filled with brown cows and the air is filled with the tinkling of cowbells. This is the Innerschweiz, made up of the three cantons of Uri, Schwyz and Unterwalden, which formed the nucleus of Switzerland almost seven centuries ago. Here one becomes keenly aware of the characteristic odor of rural Switzerland, a blend of hay and manure. The dung, which many Swiss farmers pile on the street sides of their houses, is a symbol of affluence, indicating the number of cows in a barn. This cult of manure is largely responsible for the astonishing fertility of the valleys. With only 30 per cent of its land fit for growing food crops, Switzerland in normal times manages to feed three fifths of its population.

Another aid to fertility is the humidity. The upsweeping currents of air from the valleys, cooled by mountain glaciers, drop moisture frequently. In some parts of the country, in St. Gall for instance, some rain falls during the day on 173 days a year, and here in the Innerschweiz there are frequent thunderstorms in the summer, followed by glowing rainbows.

The road north from the Innerschweiz takes one along a chain of lakes with orchards on their shores and fields of haycocks set like thimbles on a green counterpane. These give way to the old and picturesque town of Zug and then to Zurich, a bright northern city shimmering with water and light, with splashing fountains and chestnut trees and church towers with clock faces, constant reminders to bankers and merchants not to waste a minute's time. Beyond Zurich the land recedes in gentle slopes of shocked wheat and ripening vegetables to Schaffhausen and the swiftly flowing Rhine, with vineyards on its northern shore and towns with ornately frescoed houses.

FROM the Rhine villages one may drive east to misty Lake Constance and then south over grassy hills to the toylike villages of the canton of Appenzell facing into Austria. Pursuing the tumultuous Rhine into the Grisons through the towered mountain city of Chur, one passes medieval castles from which dukes battled to control the strategically important river, and then swings down to the sunny blue-watered Engadine and the glittering international resort of St. Moritz.

Or one can drive west from Schaffhausen, following the Rhine to the river city of Basel, and then along the western slopes of the Jura through rolling high pastures to Neuchâtel with its placid gull-inhabited lake, and from it across one of Switzerland's few plains to Bern. Driving south from Bern, one crosses the border between German- and French-speaking Switzerland. From the medieval-towered university town of Fribourg one continues through vineyards to Lausanne, built on steep hills above the Lake of Geneva. From Lausanne the road follows the limpid blue lake to Geneva itself, Calvin's city on the swift-flowing Rhone. Switzerland's most famous town, Geneva is also its most cosmopolitan, with foreigners making up more than one fourth of its population.

ALMOST all of the southern half of the country is mountainous, and if the mountains have helped protect Switzerland from outsiders, they have also helped preserve the ethnic variety of the Swiss themselves. A majority of the Swiss—almost four million—speak a Germanic language called Schwyzerdütsch, but virtually every canton has its own dialect of this Swiss-German tongue which the people cling to with fierce local pride. In addition, there are a million Swiss who speak French and more than half a million who speak either Italian or Romansch, a derivative of Latin spoken since Roman times in the isolated canton of the Grisons. It has been said, with only slight exaggeration, that Switzerland has as many peoples as it has valleys. In appearance the urban Swiss, the bankers and merchants of Zurich and Geneva, are as gray-flanneled and smooth-shaven as city dwellers anywhere. On the other hand, rural Swiss have preserved, with their dialects, their historical variations in dress and appearance. The most striking view of such a diverse human landscape may be found at the *Schützenfest*, a national sharpshooting contest held every five years in one or another of the major Swiss cities.

The marksmen, most of whom arrive by train, parade from the railroad station to the shooting field dressed in their cantonal costumes, bearing cantonal flags, trophies and arms—halberds, crossbows and rifles. There are blue-eyed types from the Swiss Rhineland and brawny, redheaded men from the Haslital

valley near Bern. There are supple, vivacious Suisses Romands from the shores of the Lake of Geneva and brightly costumed, black-haired, singing Italian-Swiss from the Ticino. Stern landsmen from Glarus lope as if they had for centuries carried the world on their shoulders, and bearded little herdsmen from Appenzell smoke pipes and wear yellow leather britches, flowers on their hats and a gold ring in one ear.

Most astonishing of the marchers are the terrifying men of Innerschweiz, herdsmen from above the shores of the Lake of Lucerne in the forested heart of the land. These great brawny giants, some wearing the horns of oxen, the cantonal symbol of Uri, on their heads and blowing enormous horns which sound like the lowings of bulls, are the lineal descendants of the Helvetian race whom Julius Caesar called the bravest of the Gauls.

These men are, in a sense, the aristocracy of Switzerland, the descendants of the original confederates of Uri, Schwyz and Unterwalden who, determined to preserve their ancient tribal self-government against the encroachments of medieval princes, united in 1291 in a pact of "oath comradeship." They are the "noble savages" so much admired (from a distance) by the effete courtiers of 18th Century France.

Stolid and deliberate, the men of Innerschweiz are also mystics with an obsessive love for liberty. They clung for centuries to a primitive democracy of direct popular assembly which showed the world the way to the more complex but basically similar institutions of popular initiative and referendum.

URI is the legendary home of Wilhelm Tell, Switzerland's national hero, whose statue can be seen in a dozen towns, whose life story as dramatized by the German poet Friedrich Schiller is performed every summer in the towns of Altdorf and Interlaken (and by Swiss-Americans in New Glarus, Wisconsin) and whose crossbow is the trademark of every product exported by Switzerland. To a Swiss it makes no difference that Tell probably never existed. His supposed birthplace in Bürglen is

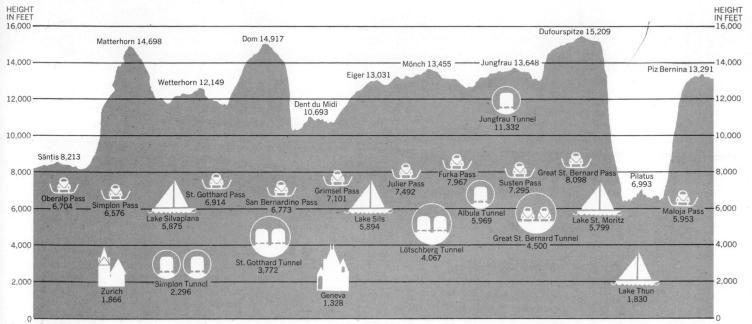

HEIGHT IN FEET 16,000

14,000

12,000

10,000

8,000

6,000

4,000

2,000

0

HEIGHT IN FEET 16,000

14,000

12,000

10,000

8,000

6,000

4,000

2,000

0

Matterhorn 14,698
Dom 14,917
Dufourspitze 15,209
Wetterhorn 12,149
Mönch 13,455 — Jungfrau 13,648
Eiger 13,031
Piz Bernina 13,291
Dent du Midi 10,693
Jungfrau Tunnel 11,332
Säntis 8,213
Furka Pass 7,967
Great St. Bernard Pass 8,098
Pilatus 6,993
Oberalp Pass 6,704
Simplon Pass 6,576
St. Gotthard Pass 6,914
San Bernardino Pass 6,773
Grimsel Pass 7,101
Julier Pass 7,492
Susten Pass 7,295
Lake Silvaplana 5,875
Lake Sils 5,894
Albula Tunnel 5,969
Maloja Pass 5,953
Lake St. Moritz 5,799
St. Gotthard Tunnel 3,772
Lötschberg Tunnel 4,067
Great St. Bernard Tunnel 4,500
Simplon Tunnel 2,296
Zurich 1,866
Geneva 1,328
Lake Thun 1,830

RELATIVE HEIGHTS of some of the best-known peaks, passes, tunnels, lakes and cities in Switzerland are shown on the stylized chart above, which shows these features without regard to their actual location. Most tunnels are for railroads (automobiles are carried on flatcars), but the Great St. Bernard Tunnel, completed in 1964, has been built for motorcars only.

marked by a chapel. Frescoed shrines stand in Altdorf, where he is said to have shot the apple from his son's head; near Flüelen, where he escaped from an Austrian boat; in the Hohle Gasse (hollow lane) near Küssnacht, where he ambushed and shot the villainous Gessler; and on the bank of the Schächen River, where a stone cross indicates the depths in which he is supposed to have drowned. Although fictitious, Tell has proved more alive than any historical Swiss. An actor who played the role for 24 summers said, "Schiller didn't create Tell. He was created by the Swiss people. Tell is a lone wolf of great strength, of deep pride and no fear. He is a warrior who is a pacifist, a peasant who is also a philosopher. He is the kind of man every Swiss would like to be."

The independence, aloof self-possession and inner loneliness which are part of the character of Tell—and of every Swiss—are also reflected in some of the country's folk music—in the vocal calls known as yodeling and in the lowing Alphorn, both of which began in ancient times, probably with the purpose of gathering the cattle. The Alphorn is not unlike in its effect another highland instrument, the Scotsman's bagpipe. However they differ in their tone, both express a wild melancholy. The sound of yodeling is supposed to have developed in imitation of the rise and fall of echoes of the human voice caused by mountain walls. To the uninitiated, the sliding arpeggios between a natural and a falsetto voice may seem absurd and even unpleasant. Many of the lyrics of the songs that accompany yodeling express a romantic longing to return to the simplicities of childhood.

THE Swiss's similarity to the Scots, also a mountain people, goes beyond their music. The Swiss, like the Scots, are often superstitious. Sudden storms, avalanches, the weird forms of rising mists and clouds, all magnified by the intense solitude of the highlands, inspire belief in the supernatural and a brooding preoccupation with sin. It is no accident that the puritanical Calvinist faith which first took root in Geneva flourished next in Scotland, to which it was carried by John Knox and other disciples of Calvin. Both Swiss and Scots are known for being careful with their pennies, and this concern for money was abetted by Calvin's notion that poverty in this world was a sign of damnation in the next, and wealth in this world a sign of salvation. Such a theological justification of materialism, spread by Calvinism through England and thence to America, became a moral basis for the capitalist civilization of the West. It is probably not a coincidence that the leading 19th Century steelmaking millionaires in the United States included a man of Swiss ancestry, Henry Clay Frick, and the Scotch Presbyterian Andrew Carnegie.

Nor is it an accident that 20th Century Swiss are among the great bankers of the world. During all the wars, revolutions and other crises that have shaken Europe in the last 100 years, the banks of Switzerland have stood solid. When World War II ended, Zurich's principal avenue, the Bahnhofstrasse, was the banking center of Continental Europe and a world-wide deposit vault. The Swiss love other people's money almost as much as their own, and they have never cared particularly whose money they husband. Nazi fortunes were secured behind the red-geranium window boxes of the great banks, and Latin American dictators have stashed away their piles there. Guatemala's dictator Jacobo Arbenz, whose father was Swiss, was reunited with his stolen money in Switzerland after his exile in 1954, and it is no secret that Argentina's Juan Perón hoarded his loot in Swiss banks.

SWITZERLAND'S puritanism makes the country kin to England and America, and this no doubt is one reason, along with good plumbing and a general air of honesty, why many tourists from those countries feel more at ease in Switzerland than in other European countries. A Swiss, whose puritanism, whether he is a Catholic or Protestant, is his national heritage, believes that nothing is given man, that the temporal blessings of life are the rewards of virtue and hard work—which is itself the first of virtues. This conviction is shared alike by Zurich banker and Alpine herdsman. A Swiss's passion for work, his feeling of guilt over idleness, is almost a neurosis, for he is certain there can be no pleasure without effort and he distrusts what comes without pain. He knows he is living in the most comfortable and most peaceful land in the world because he, with his canny head and dexterous hands, has made it so.

Contemptuous foreigners like to say that the Swiss are dull functionaries, clods without refinement or artistic imagination. It is not true, of course, for Switzerland's writers, painters and composers are well known. But Switzerland's greatest, most enduring works of art are a system of government by which a complexity of racial, linguistic and religious groups rule themselves in peace, and a healthy economy buttressed by the world's most stable currency.

DISTRUSTING change, the Swiss cling loyally to the ancient traditions. "We wish to be free as our fathers," Schiller quotes the nation's founders as saying. Free as their fathers—neither more nor less. This innate conservatism makes the Swiss less rabid for personal liberty than, for example, the French or the English. The German poet Goethe found the Swiss little better off than slaves, despite their democratic government. Of Swiss freedom he said, "Free, these prosperous burghers in their closed cities? Free, these poor devils on their cliffs and rocks? The things one can make people believe! . . . They did make themselves free once . . . [but] now they sit behind their walls, caught by their habits and their laws, their haggish gossip and their philistinism." The British historian Edward Gibbon, as aware as Goethe of the difference between political and social freedoms, said there was only one thing that the free Swiss lacked and that was freedom.

What the Swiss in their peasant wisdom have grasped perhaps better than poets and historians is that, especially in a country as small as theirs, the individual must to some degree forego his desire for complete personal freedom in the interests of the community. The Swiss know that an individual's liberties are safe only when the liberties of every other man are protected. Freedom of discussion, the principle upon which their democracy operates, is, however, a national passion. *"Mir rede mit enand,"* they say. "We discuss with one another."

A Swiss is a citizen not of a state or nation, but of his commune. He is first a man from the commune of Sion, then from the canton of Valais and only incidentally a Swiss. There are 3,095 communes in the Swiss Confederation, each with its own governing body and its own laws, and it is by these and the laws of a canton that a Swiss is ruled. With the mobility that follows industrialization, however, only a fourth of today's Swiss live in the commune of which they are citizens, with the result that the Confederation has been slowly broadening its powers.

Proud to be citizens of their communes and cantons, the Swiss are reluctant to extend this citizenship to outsiders. In much the same way, Switzerland is reluctant to lose a single native subject, and emigrés who become citizens of other lands are still considered subjects of their communes and have, on occasion, received Swiss draft notices. A fourth-generation American on a visit to his ancestral village of Elm discovered that his birth, and those of all his living relatives, had been officially recorded in the cantonal courthouse.

THERE is no proletariat in Switzerland and no established gentry, only farmers and urban bourgeoisie. There are differences of wealth, of course, but they are carefully hidden. A millionaire banker will ride the bus to work. A laborer will tend his vegetable garden, take pride in his window boxes full of geraniums and maintain a boat on the lake. The common prosperity is deliberately extended to all, and everyone aspires to be middle class. A nation of bourgeois, the Swiss, however, are not interested in becoming like one another. Instead of promoting, or even desiring, conformism, the Swiss are eager to maintain and enjoy their personal peculiarities. Diversity and human individuality are considered strengths, indeed the life blood of the nation.

There is no sentimental idealism in this, no ennobling love for man. It is just more practical, the Swiss have discovered, to let the other man go his own way. In fact, a Swiss tends to be rather suspicious and to keep to himself. Communal feuds have continued for centuries, and the epithets which cantons have for one

another are a part of the language. Zurichers consider the Bernese boors as clumsy as their bears, and the Bernese look on Zurichers as shrewd city-slickers. Both consider the people of Glarus intractable rustics comparable to American hillbillies, Baselers intellectual snobs, Wallisers pugnacious quarrelers and the Genevese proprietors of a Sodom or Gomorrah. The popular cabaret actor Walter Morath, describing "the land of brotherly hate," says, "The simple truth is that we love foreigners because we detest ourselves so much. It is easy to love humanity. It is your neighbor that is so hard to bear. The people of Lausanne have nothing against Australians. They only dislike the people of Geneva."

Rather than feign a reciprocal affection, the Swiss prefer to control their innate antagonisms. A canton never officially declares itself Protestant or Catholic, French or German or Italian. An astonishing example of Swiss tolerance is a score of *Simultan-Kirchen* (simultaneous churches) in which both Catholics and Protestants worship. By tacitly agreeing to disagree, the Swiss turn religious, cultural and linguistic differences, which cause riots and insurrections in a country like Belgium, into stabilizing forces in their union.

TO preserve this union the Swiss are prepared to fight. The Swiss do not have an army; they *are* an army. Switzerland is the only country in the world where the entire able-bodied male population is under constant alert to mobilize. Every man is a soldier from his 20th to his 60th year. After a period of basic training in his youth he remains for many years in the active reserve, devoting several weeks each year to refresher maneuvers. Such a military program is a vital instrument for education and a perpetual reaffirmation of democracy. Friendships formed in the *Rekrutenschule* are maintained for life, and it is not uncommon for a factory owner to bend a convivial elbow with an old army comrade who may be a taxi-driver. Rifle marksmanship is a national sport in the land of Wilhelm Tell, and in every rural valley on a Sunday morning the pealing of church bells is punctuated by the staccato bang-bang of rifles.

One of the most nationalistic peoples in the world, the Swiss are also one of the most international, paradoxically cherishing human solidarity almost as much as political insularity. Swiss neutrality has been often misunderstood by the world. Sometimes praised, it has also been criticized by the governments of larger countries. Long famous as fierce mercenary soldiers, the Swiss nevertheless learned from experience centuries ago that neutrality was a condition of their national survival, no more and no less. Containing within its boundaries the bloods, cultures and languages of Germany, France and Italy, Switzerland, had it taken sides in any of Europe's modern conflicts, would probably have been torn apart. It is because of Switzerland's neutrality, plus the country's central location, that it was chosen as the site of the League of Nations and of many United Nations relief organizations.

A PEOPLE so free of poverty, economic stress and political tension as the Swiss should be sublimely happy. To a tourist entering from France or Italy it appears that they are. Once the frontier is crossed everything seems cleaner and better organized, and the people are politely amiable. They wear clothes of excellent material, the furniture and appliances in their houses are new and modern, their food markets overflow with abundance. The visitor gets the impression he is entering a world of serenity, a world in which laws are respected, where the wheels of society are oiled, where the people concentrate on their mutual well-being with a single-minded zeal. An irreverent Frenchman compared the country to an efficient and contented colony of ants.

Entomologists tell us that even ant colonies have nervous breakdowns, and Switzerland's tranquility is not as real as it seems. A Swiss's chronic worrying and habitual grousing hardly indicate a happy state of mind. Switzerland ranks among the world's leaders in the rate of both suicide and divorce. Murder, big-time holdups and burglaries are infrequent, but the kinds of crime for which the Swiss seem to have a special disposition are sexual, a fact which will surprise no student of puritan psychology. In the cities, prostitution and perversion, both tolerated, flourish.

It is not surprising that a Swiss, Dr. Carl Jung, was able to move the fountainhead of psychiatry from Vienna to Zurich. An analyst says that the malignant gloom and pessimism which are symptoms of the *malaise suisse* are characteristics of mountain people. Living in constant intimacy with mountains seems to result in a sort of national inferiority complex, which in the case of Switzerland may be abetted by its disinvolvement in the world's crises. Said this analyst: "We have no national upheavals upon which to externalize our emotions. Business is good. We don't fight wars. There is nothing to unite us to each other in a common effort. We're unhappy and we don't know why. Material well-being reduces a man's toleration of set-backs, his ability to go down and come up again. He worries how long all these good things will last."

There is no doubt that intense self-control and national discipline bring on strain. But Switzerland, which in 1963 celebrated its 672nd anniversary as a democracy, has survived largely through just such discipline and control. Having long ago established the terms of its survival, it has clung to them without compromise and without weakness. As a living example of man's successful triumph over nature—farming steep slopes, carving out roads and tunnels, harnessing waterfalls and electrifying railroads—and indeed, of man's capacity to control his own stormy nature, Switzerland has rendered great service to the world and to human civilization.

T HE existence of a nation as diversified and at the same time as united as the Swiss is proof that peaceful cooperation between dissimilar peoples is not impossible, that man has reason to hope that in time he will be able to bring reason to bear on all his dealings.

A silvery, foaming cascade of the Stäuben River descends hundreds of feet into the Schächen Valley in the Alps far below Klausen Pass.

A Harmonious Blending of Setting and Structure

The variations of climate and of topography in Switzerland provide the small area with magnificent scenery and stunning contrasts. To accommodate their dwellings to the varied settings, Swiss builders have developed a wide range of architectural styles. Rough-hewn Alpine chalets cling to sheer drops, midland farmhouses ramble freely and stolidly across broad, open territory, and villas in the south form a complement to the cypresses of the Italian lakes.

ETERNAL SNOW, glistening brilliantly on the peaks of the Bernese Alps *(opposite)*, gleams above the deeply shaded valley of the Simplon Pass *(foreground)*. The highway through the pass dates from the early 1800s, when Napoleon ordered it built to help maintain effective control over his new empire.

VELVETY MEADOW provides pasturage for cows in the valley of the Vispa River *(right)*, a tributary of the Rhone. The town of Visperterminen, which is 4,397 feet above sea level, is low enough to permit farming and stock raising, yet high enough to make its nearby vineyards the highest found in Europe.

CROWDED QUAYS of Zurich, Switzerland's largest city, accommodate the heavy boat traffic on the Limmat River. The two churches *(background)* were first built in the 13th Century.

STEEP SLOPES rise dramatically from the Lake of Thun *(right)* in the canton of Bern. Eleven miles long and ringed with chalets and villages, the lake is one of many centers of Swiss sailing.

ITALIANATE VILLAS on the Lake of Lugano in the southern canton of Ticino hover in twilight. Not far from Lombardy, the Ticino is the only canton where Italian is the principal tongue.

MEDIEVAL TOWN of Bremgarten, with its population of 3,200, lies in the lower Reuss valley in Aargau. Since the 13th Century, water wheels have turned mills in the town.

ALLEGORICAL FRESCO *(opposite)* graces the Inn of the Sun, one of many extravagantly decorated houses in Stein am Rhein, a town close to the German border.

MASSIVE FARMHOUSE showing the architectural style of the Bernese Mittelland *(left)* belongs to the family which is raking and pitching hay into a horse-drawn wagon.

Die Sonne, Fürst, lafs mir herein
Der Menschen Glanz ist leerer Schein

Gasthof zur Sonne

2

Warriors and Mediators

SWITZERLAND was brought into history by Julius Caesar. But many millennia before Caesar's brazen legions marched, the land had been inhabited. Cave dwellers may have lived in the valleys as many as 50,000 years ago, and they were followed by a Neolithic people who fished on the shores of Switzerland's many lakes, perching their huts on piles driven into the swampy shores.

During the Iron Age several tribes of barbaric Celts overran the area and one of them, the Helvetii, stayed. By 500 B.C. these Helvetians seem to have shared the land with a wild tribe called the Raeti, from northern Italy. They were not destined to share the land in peace. Soon restless and powerful Germanic tribes from north of the Rhine began to press relentlessly southward.

As these tribes pushed deeper and deeper into Switzerland, the Helvetians became alarmed and finally conceived the astonishing plan of a mass migration. In 58 B.C., a great column of men, women and children, with their cattle and provisions, started westward toward what is today southern France, their goal the mouth of the Garonne River and the Atlantic coast.

It was this attempted tribal relocation that ushered Switzerland onto the stage of world history. Southern France was a Roman province and Caesar was understandably reluctant to have this disrupting human tide cross his territory. He rushed 700 miles from Rome to Geneva in eight days, marshaled six legions and defeated the Alpine tribesmen in a battle near the present-day French city of Autun. After the defeat, Caesar ordered the Helvetii to stay home.

To see that they did, and to hold off any further invasions by Germanic tribes, Caesar left several military garrisons in Switzerland. Over the succeeding centuries the troops and the Roman governors established Roman law and built towns with palaces, temples and amphitheaters. They introduced cherries and chickens to Helvetian agriculture and improved cattle breeds and the cultivation of vineyards. Their most enduring enterprise was the construction of roads with which they crisscrossed the country, including a road over the Great St. Bernard Pass which assured permanent communication between Italy and the north.

THE Romans retained control of Switzerland until the beginning of the Fifth Century A.D., when they were forced to withdraw their legions to help defend Italy from the Huns and other barbarians. With the Romans gone, two Germanic tribes gradually took over Switzerland. The Burgundians moved in from the west. The Alemanni, invading from the north, gradually pushed the Burgundians to the Sarine River, which became the border between the two and established permanently the division which still exists today between Switzerland's French- and German-speaking peoples.

In the Sixth Century both tribes came under Frankish rule, and the country eventually became a part of Charlemagne's Holy Roman Empire. After Charlemagne died in 814, his descendants fell to bickering among themselves and Switzerland was once again divided, this time between two of Charlemagne's grandsons who ruled upper Burgundy and Germany. In 888, a minor despot named Rudolf seized part of the old Burgundian territories and had himself crowned ruler, and for 150 years the greater part of today's Switzerland had a king. Then, in 1032, when the last of this line of Burgundian kings died, Helvetia fell to Conrad II, the ruler of Germany and the Holy Roman Empire. For the next four centuries most of the country, like the greater part of feudal Europe, was a loose collection of fiefs, controlled by bishops and ducal families who levied their own taxes and dispensed their own law, but acknowledged fealty to the Holy Roman Emperor.

EVENTUALLY this division of rule was more than the liberty-loving peasants in the interior of Helvetia could stomach. They were willing to acknowledge the ultimate authority of the German Emperor, but the bailiffs and tax gatherers who were their immediate overlords interfered with their ancient processes of self-government. This communal government, inherited from their Germanic forebears, was a necessity for people attempting to wrest a living from steep, boulder-strewn fields. Cooperation was essential if pastures were to be protected from overgrazing, use of the water supply regulated, the market value of produce kept at profitable levels. In the remote valleys of Uri and Schwyz and Unterwalden, the citizens determined to liberate themselves from all feudal obligations and become free men.

In 1291, when the Holy Roman Emperor, Rudolf of Habsburg, died, the Helvetians decided their moment had come. On August 1, before a new emperor could be elected by a council of German princes, the elders of the three small states met on a tiny heath known as the Rütli on the shores of the Lake of Lucerne and negotiated an "eternal pact." They declared their right to local self-government, promised one another assistance against any encroachment upon these rights and committed future generations to an alliance that was to "endure forever." The pact was the beginning of the Everlasting League and the foundation of the Swiss Confederation. The forest meadow, the Rütli, accessible only by boat or by foot down a steep trail, is Switzerland's most venerated patriotic shrine. Every school child is required to make at least one pilgrimage to it.

In the century that followed the signing of the Eternal Pact, this nucleus of free Switzerland maintained and even enlarged itself by a combination of hard fighting and clever scheming. Of great aid were endless dynastic struggles over who should sit on the throne of the Holy Roman Empire. The self-ruling Swiss confederates swore allegiance to whichever pretender seemed most likely to leave them alone. When these maneuvers failed, the burly mountaineers picked up their weapons and fought, defeating Austrian armies led by members of the Habsburg dynasty in three violent and crucial battles: at Morgarten in 1315, at Sempach in 1386 and at Näfels in 1388.

After Morgarten, the rebels celebrated the victory by reaffirming their pledge of collective security with the Pact of Brunnen. In the next 40 years five new states—Lucerne, Zurich, Glarus, Zug and Bern—were added to the union. Known as the Confederation of the Leagues of Upper Germany, it came to be called by the name of one of the founding cantons, Schwyz, or Switzerland.

THROUGHOUT the next century, the 15th, the number of cantons remained unchanged. This was due partly to ingrained Swiss conservatism and partly to the fear on the part of the original rural states that the increasingly wealthy and populous cities would dominate the league. During this time the "Switzers" were enlarging their reputation as soldiers and becoming a power to be reckoned with in Europe. Caught between the ambitions of Louis XI of France and Charles the Bold, the powerful Duke of Burgundy, the Swiss twice defeated Charles's armies in 1476, and in 1477, Swiss mercenary troops marched to the aid of the Duke of Lorraine at Nancy, where Charles was slain. Once this common enemy was conquered, the Swiss immediately began to brawl among themselves, and the question of admitting two city cantons, Fribourg and Solothurn, into the league almost led to civil war.

Fighting seemed imminent and unavoidable when, providentially, a saint appeared to quell the flaring tempers. He was a hermit known as Nicholas of Flue who, in a dramatic appeal to the diet at Stans in 1481, was able to persuade the confederates to settle their differences by compromise rather than by war. The towns should be admitted, he advised, provided they abandoned their separate alliances and remained neutral in any conflict which might divide the original eight cantons. On the same terms two more towns, Basel and Schaffhausen, and rural Appenzell were soon taken into the league. The great mediator, who had fathered 10 children before he fled the world into his cave, is credited also with fathering Switzerland's famous neutrality. He was later canonized and is Switzerland's patron saint.

THOUGH they were to take in no new cantons for 300 years, and then only at the instigation of Napoleon, the belligerent Swiss continued to seize territories which were later to become cantons. Pacts and treaties circled the Confederation with a number of new allies. The Grisons, for example, itself a confederation of three separate leagues, was such an associated district. Under obligation to supply troops whenever needed, these protectorates greatly increased the Confederation's military strength.

The Swiss's fame as ferocious "tamers of kings" continued to spread. Within 35 years they defeated three of Europe's most powerful monarchs. Having crushed Charles the Bold, they took the measure of Maximilian I, who wished to re-establish the rights of the Holy Roman Empire, such as levying taxes, in Switzerland. Shortly afterward, in 1512, the Swiss, siding with Pope Julius II against Louis XII of France, drove a French army out of northern Italy. Although they suffered a crushing defeat three years later at Marignano, the Swiss had proved their military prowess and they came to be in great demand as mercenary troops.

Historians like to call this era Switzerland's heroic age. After Marignano the Swiss nation suddenly, and finally, curbed its hunger for

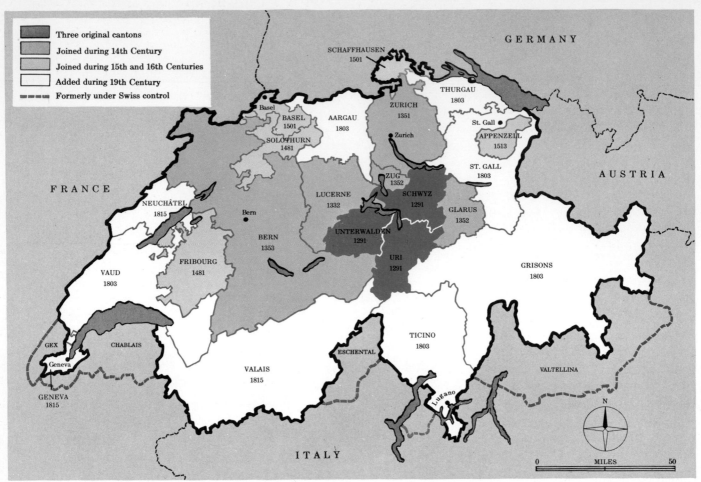

Three original cantons
Joined during 14th Century
Joined during 15th and 16th Centuries
Added during 19th Century
Formerly under Swiss control

GERMANY

SCHAFFHAUSEN
1501

THURGAU
1803

ZURICH
1351

St. Gall

APPENZELL
1513

AUSTRIA

Basel

BASEL
1501

AARGAU
1803

SOLOTHURN
1481

• Zurich

ZUG
1352

ST. GALL
1803

FRANCE

NEUCHÂTEL
1815

LUCERNE
1332

SCHWYZ
1291

GLARUS
1352

• Bern

UNTERWALDEN
1291

GRISONS
1803

BERN
1353

URI
1291

FRIBOURG
1481

VAUD
1803

TICINO
1803

GEX

Geneva

CHABLAIS

ESCHENTAL

VALTELLINA

VALAIS
1815

Lugano

GENEVA
1815

N

ITALY

0   MILES   50

SWITZERLAND'S GROWTH began with the pact made by Uri, Schwyz and Unterwalden in 1291. This group was later joined by other areas, eventually forming the Confederation existing today. The dates indicate when the cantons came into the Confederation. Only 22 cantons are shown, but technically there are 25, three being divided into two administrative parts.

new territory and ceased intervening in foreign wars. National neutrality did not, however, halt hired soldiering. Mercenary service, like almost everything else in Switzerland's history, was a practical expediency. In a country poor in land and natural resources, it became an economic necessity, especially in the forest cantons. Not only were young men assured food and adventure, they were able to send money home to support their families. War became the small, impoverished nation's first important export. Swiss troops, individual volunteers or whole regiments, have served in virtually every war of the last five centuries, including the American Civil War and World War I.

No sooner had the Swiss decided to eschew further foreign ventures than new and bitter storms began to brew up at home. In Zurich the people's priest of Great Minster Cathedral,

Ulrich Zwingli, basing his sermons on the Gospel, was preaching against fasting, saint worship and the celibacy of priests. Like Martin Luther in Germany, he openly fought the Roman Catholic Church's sale of indulgences. Zwingli's 67 theses and Luther's famous 95 theses agreed on most points, although one basic difference in the interpretation of the communion involved the two reformers in acrimonious dispute.

By preaching that the congregation, and not a priestly hierarchy, was the true governing body of the Church, and by proposing to unify church and state into a sort of collective socialism, Zwingli was a revolutionary not only in theology, as was Luther, but also in politics. His ideas won the support of the city cantons of Zurich, Bern, Basel and Schaffhausen, and were invincibly opposed by the six original rural cantons and by urban Lucerne. War broke out between the two factions and Zwingli was killed in battle in 1531.

The next, and as far as Western civilization is concerned, the most decisive, chapter of Swiss history did not occur inside the Confederation at all but in Geneva, which, although Swiss in spirit and sympathies, was not to become a Swiss canton until 1815. Geneva, at the beginning of the 16th Century, had been under the rule of the House of Savoy for more than a century. Tiring of this Savoyard domination, the Genevese determined to fight for their independence and turned to the Swiss Confederation for aid. The confederates soon found a pretext under which to enter Geneva, and in 1530 forced the reigning Duke of Savoy to renounce his rights to the city.

BERN, which became Geneva's principal ally, had accepted the Reformation in 1528. Under the influence of Bern and its persuasive preachers, the Genevese came to accept the new faith themselves. This conversion had little to do with religious considerations. The Genevese, some 16,000 of them, were worldly merchants and artisans who cherished the pleasures of the flesh. They drank freely of the wines produced on the shores of their lake. Men were expected to have mistresses, although, with characteristic prudence, the Genevese had enacted a law forbidding married men to keep more than one mistress at a time.

The Genevan reform was, then, not entirely the result of changed belief or a new purity of heart but of political expediency. Looking on it as a liberation from authority, the merry Genevese turned their reformation into a riot. After the new faith was proclaimed in 1536, they invaded their cathedral, tore down everything except the walls, and brought in dogs and mules to befoul what was left. Defrocked priests danced on their robes.

One of the leaders of Geneva's fight for independence from Savoy, a former Cluniac prior named François Bonivard, was captured by the soldiers of Savoy and imprisoned in the dungeon of Chillon castle, where three centuries later Lord Byron found Bonivard's name carved in rock and immortalized his story in a long romantic poem. Liberated from the "damp vault's dayless gloom," Bonivard emerged to find the once gay city a gloomy fortress of purity in which his third wife was to be sentenced for adultery, sewn into a bag and thrown into the Rhone.

What had happened was that John Calvin had arrived in Geneva and become its master. One can feel, even today, the dour spirit of the epoch by standing before Geneva's austere Reformation Monument and looking up into Calvin's haggard, ascetic, bearded face, at his bony hands, both of them holding an open Bible. It is all there: the Jehovistic rage, the humorless inhumanity, the intractable will. Finding what seemed to him a city besieged by Satan, Calvin, who had been exiled from his native France for his heretical opinions, set out to transform Geneva into a city of God. His method was to renovate human character by force. Every citizen was required by law to attend church twice on Sunday and to be at home by nine in the evening. Card playing, wearing jewelry and eating rich foods were punishable crimes. A consistory of ministers and elders met every Thursday to pass sentence according to these new and ferocious laws, and the public registers were filled with entries such as this: "May 20, 1537: A wife having gone out last Sunday with her hair looser than it is proper . . . they put into jail the mistress, the ladies who accompanied her and the one who combed her hair."

WHILE Zwingli had built a church to function within the state, Calvin's church *was* the state. In his Holy Commonwealth the majority of the citizens were irrevocably doomed to Hell by Calvin's doctrine of predestination. To the remainder, destined for saintliness as was Calvin himself, fell the role of judging and chastising the unworthy in this life as well. With his reformation, Calvin succeeded in turning Geneva into a Protestant Vatican, which he ruled more imperiously than any pope ever ruled Rome. The city became a seminary for a new breed of apostles who carried Calvin's doctrines abroad.

Many historians believe that Calvin, more than any other man, made the modern era possible. In a generally libertine era, they point out, Calvinism conferred on humanity freedom of action through restraint. Calvin's new cardinal virtue of hard work, applied to newly saved stores of capital, produced in due time the industrial world. Calvinism shortly became the doctrine of the reformed churches of France, Holland, Scotland, Hungary, and part of North America, where it was carried by the Puritan Pilgrims. The moral character of the New World was formed when Calvin arrived in Geneva.

FOR three centuries after Calvin, Switzerland remained a warring camp of religious factions. In 1597 the canton of Appenzell split into halves: Catholic Inner Rhoden and Protestant Ausser Rhoden. For a time it appeared that a similar division would have to be made in all Switzerland. There were for a time, in fact, two Confederations: a Catholic one with a government in Lucerne and a Protestant one with a government in Aarau. However, despite internal divisions that remained deep and dangerous, Switzerland enjoyed a long period of comparative peace and prosperity during much of the 17th Century and throughout the 18th. The country's complete independence from the Holy Roman Empire was recognized in 1648 by the treaty which ended the Thirty Years' War, and the Swiss celebrated with an orgy of hard work which expanded the country's industries. The sciences flourished to a point where Geneva's Academy became the envy of Europe and America.

This happy state of affairs was shattered by that great European convulsion, the French Revolution, and its aftermath of wars. For some years Switzerland managed to remain neutral, even though feelings within the country ran high, at first for the Revolution's libertarian ideals and then against the excesses of the Terror. However, with each victory of its revolutionary army the French became more greedy and by 1797, when Napoleon had conquered northern Italy, Switzerland, with its strategic central location, seemed an irresistible morsel. The French Army cut through an inadequate Swiss defense and Bern fell on March 5, 1798.

The ancient Confederation was dissolved and Switzerland was made into a dependent Helvetic Republic. The occupation gave the French all they hoped for: control of the Alpine passes, a large treasury of Swiss bullion to finance Napoleon's campaigns and several regiments of soldiers. The results were not so fine for Switzerland. Austrian and Russian troops, pursuing the French in 1799, turned the country into a battleground, and the last anarchic revolutionary governments in Paris totally mismanaged Swiss affairs. Napoleon, finally recognizing that centuries of history could not be ignored, dictated an Act of Mediation in 1802 after he had assumed control of France. It established a new Swiss Confederation and added to the 13 original cantons six new ones: Aargau, the Grisons, St. Gall, Thurgau, Ticino and Vaud.

THE Swiss wisely stayed aloof from the rest of the Napoleonic wars, and in 1815 the Congress of Vienna recognized the perpetual neutrality, independence and inviolability of Switzerland. Three old allies—Valais, Neuchâtel and Geneva—were added to the Confederation, bringing the total number of cantons to 22. Three of these cantons are divided in two, making the 25 cantons of present-day Switzerland.

Soon after 1815, the Swiss reverted to old ways, bickering and fighting among themselves. Cantons drew up their own laws, flew their own flags and minted their own coins. Religious differences were intensified until in 1845, seven Catholic cantons formed a separate league called the Sonderbund which the federal Diet ordered to disband. When the rebels refused, the Diet ordered the federal troops to attack. Switzerland's civil war of 1847 was not, however, a very serious affair, lasting only 25 days and costing a total of 128 lives.

The next year a new Swiss federal Constitution was drawn up. Patterning some of its provisions on the Constitution of the United States, it granted autonomy to cantons but not the right to make alliances with one another or with foreign states. It established a common currency and a single postal administration, and it abolished all customs barriers except national ones. The new Confederation adopted as its flag a white cross against a red field because it had been carried by troops fighting for Swiss freedom 500 years earlier.

Its domestic turmoil finally resolved, Switzerland was free to develop its international role. In 1862 the Geneva humanitarian Henri Dunant published his *Un Souvenir de Solferino*, an eloquent account of the suffering of the wounded in the wars that attended the unification of Italy. Largely as a result of Dunant's book, the Red Cross was founded in Geneva during the following year. Adhering to their strict neutrality through the Franco-Prussian War, the Swiss bent their efforts to enlarging industry and improving communications. In 1872 work was begun on the Gotthard tunnel, the most important transit artery in Europe; 34 years later the Simplon, the longest tunnel in Europe, was opened. In 1914 Switzerland issued a declaration stating its intent not to depart in any way from "the principles of neutrality so dear to the Swiss people." This declaration was respected and six years later the London Declaration reaffirmed Switzerland's neutrality.

RECOGNIZED by international law, neutrality was now a permanent force free to grow into a positive creative strength. Geneva was chosen as the seat of the League of Nations, which Switzerland joined with special concessions freeing it from military obligations. With the tragic failure of the League and the coming of World War II, invasion from the north once more seemed imminent. Determined to resist, General Henri Guisan, Swiss commander-in-chief, assembled his officers on the hallowed Rütli meadow and announced that Switzerland would resist any aggression with armed force. The Swiss strategy included full mobilization, the manning of all the extensive Alpine fortifications and the mining of such main arteries as the Gotthard tunnel, which, should the need arise, would be blown up.

This final move, perhaps more than any other consideration, kept Hitler out of Switzerland. To have conquered a Switzerland with its fine communications system in ruins would have been a hollow victory. During the war a Swiss Navy of 43 Red Cross ships carried 470,000 tons of relief supplies to belligerent countries, and a central tracing agency in Geneva answered up to 70,000 letters a day relating to war prisoners and missing civilians. The Swiss opened up their homes to war orphans and in the canton of Appenzell, the Pestalozzi Children's Village was built to provide a refuge and education for homeless children.

THE United Nations' system of collective security has prevented Switzerland from joining that organization. Nevertheless the Swiss have joined many U.N. relief organizations, several of which are located in Geneva. In addition, the Swiss have acted as diplomatic caretakers in innumerable cases. Their embassy in Havana looks after American interests there. They supervised the exchanges of prisoners after the Korean War and they sent a team of experts—accountants, doctors, technicians—to the Congo to try to help restore order after the Belgians left.

More and more, however, the Swiss are making it apparent that their neutrality is not a neutrality of opinion. "Swiss people can never be ideologically neutral," said Dr. Kurt Müller, a political editor of the *Neue Zürcher Zeitung*. "In their soul, by their culture and their economy, they are firmly committed to the West. But the spirit of our neutrality is traditional and it will not be abrogated." What Victor Hugo said a century ago seems more true today than ever: "In history Switzerland will have the last word."

Celebrating a Vigorous Diversity

Local loyalties are deep and binding in Switzerland. A Swiss, if asked where he is from, may very well say Uri, or Glarus, and then only casually mention that this is a part of Switzerland. The 25 cantons—which are like states or provinces—have distinct personalities of their own. Although Independence Day can evoke an unembarrassed display of banners, patriotism toward the nation never detracts from loyalty to the canton. The leaders who in 1291 formed an Everlasting League of three central states would be pleased to see that it has lasted so well and expanded so much. But they might be even more pleased to find the individual cantons enthusiastically maintaining their ancient customs, their architectural distinctions and their characteristic crafts.

MEDIEVAL COSTUMES are worn by contestants preparing to board a bus during the *Schützenfest,* a marksmanship contest held once every five years to select the nation's best shooters.

EMBLAZONED FLAGS of shooting clubs and cantons are held by sashed officials at the end of a parade through Zurich, the city that played host to the 1963 championship matches.

BEARDED MOUNTAINEERS wearing the colors of Uri wait for the parade to start. The Swiss fondness for shooting recalls the centuries when they were Europe's most noted warriors.

FEDERAL OFFICIALS from Bern arrive in Appenzell, capital of the Roman Catholic half of Appenzell canton, for ceremonies celebrating the area's anniversary. During the Reformation the canton was divided in half, each half with its capital.

GREETING COMMITTEE of women is dressed in the hand-embroidered material for which the canton is famous *(opposite)*. They gather at the train station to meet dignitaries coming from Herisau, capital of the Protestant half of Appenzell canton.

HIGH POINT of the holiday is a parade *(right)* in honor of Appenzell's 450 years as a member of the Swiss Confederation. The military escort, in regional uniforms, passes beneath the standing bear flag *(top)*, which shows the canton's coat of arms.

RELIGION is a private matter in a nation almost equally divided between Catholics and Protestants

CATHOLIC SANCTUARY, the famous Benedictine abbey of Einsiedeln in the canton of Schwyz draws pilgrims from all over Europe *(left)*. Even though Einsiedeln has been a holy place since the Ninth Century, its most prominent buildings are lavish edifices in the Baroque style which date from the 18th Century.

PROTESTANT MONUMENT that was erected in Geneva in 1917 to the Reformation *(opposite)* portrays *(left to right):* Guillaume Farel, an early Protestant leader; John Calvin, who established his theocracy in 16th Century Geneva; Theodore de Beza, a Calvinist theologian; and the Scottish reformer, John Knox.

Stationed behind a desk with closed-circuit television, a partner in a private bank in Zurich supervises a Stock Exchange transaction. Swiss

bankers play the role assumed by stockbrokers in other countries.

3

The Rewards of Faith and Hard Work

"JESUS taught us that man cannot live by God and Mammon both," said a prominent Swiss with a twinkle in his eyes, "but we Swiss prove Jesus wrong. We can."

Switzerland's worship of the golden calf was afforded theological sanction by John Calvin. Scorning the Catholic and Lutheran disdain of trade and banking, the reformer openly advocated the accumulation of riches. Money is one of God's gifts to man, and therefore man must save money for God, whose administrator he is. He must account for every farthing.

From such an ideology modern capitalism drew fresh impetus, says the historian Erich Kahler. With Calvinism, he says, business enterprise became the ethic of living, and the transcendence of economic man was complete. "The power and the glory of God were replaced by the power and the glory of goods. The result was capitalistic man, who no longer enjoys his existence as an individual, who no longer enjoys the fruits of his labors but consumes his strength and his energies in impersonal mammoth enterprises."

It was Protestant refugees fleeing persecution in Catholic France and Italy who, in the 16th and 17th Centuries, brought new industries and new capital into Switzerland. As far back as the Middle Ages the poor, small country had been unable to support its population. Possessing little but a labor force, the Swiss learned early how to sell their services. The first service they sold was military—between the 15th and 19th Centuries some two million Swiss fought in foreign armies. Returning to their mountains with considerable foreign capital and a knowledge of foreign markets, the battle veterans became gifted merchants.

GRADUALLY the Swiss turned from exporting men and exported goods instead. Swiss industry is the offspring of a double tradition—the artisan skill and ingenuity of the upland peasants and the scientific abilities developed in the Protestant refugee towns. Switzerland had three great advantages: limitless water power, skilled laborers and control of mountain passes that were important to much European commerce. The country's great disadvantage, the absence of coal and oil, turned out to be an advantage, for without fuel for heavy industry Switzerland was spared the "satanic mills" of England's smoky Midlands or of America's Pittsburgh that proved one of the chief blights of the Industrial Revolution.

Instead the Swiss have made a specialty of luxury and semiluxury products which require a minimum of fuel or materials and a maximum of skills, such as watches and jewelry, precision machinery, silks and laces, medicines and fine foods. Ninety-five per cent of the cost of a Swiss watch, for instance, represents skilled labor, and only five per cent covers materials. The Swiss challenge to such industrial giants as the United States, Germany and Japan is quality. Names like Rolex, Omega and Oerlikon are known all over the world.

The greatest Swiss *Meisterwerk* of all is the economy itself, as sensitively balanced and as precise in its functioning as a good Swiss watch. Agriculture is being displaced so that today, despite travel posters still promising handsome cows and winsome milkmaids, less than 12 per cent of the Swiss population lives on the land, and Switzerland is, with Belgium and England, one of the most intensely industrialized countries in Europe. A pauper land in natural resources, it has doubled its population in the last 100 years without any expansion of territory, and has provided its people with one of the highest standards of living and with the hardest currency in the world. "We are simply bearing out Calvin," said a Swiss in jest. "God is rewarding our virtue with prosperity."

Switzerland's first large industry, and the mother of most of its other industries, was textiles. Zurich was a silk-producing center in medieval times. St. Gall was known for lace and Appenzell for embroideries. In 1895 almost 43 per cent of all Swiss industrial workers were producing textiles. In this century the industry has declined to a third of what it once was.

IT was the requirements of the textile industry during Napoleon's blockade of England, then chief producer of textile machines, which spurred Switzerland's engineering industry. Today machinery and electrical equipment account for 35 per cent of Swiss exports. Swiss diesels drive ocean vessels and the locomotives on the state railways of England, France, Spain and Japan. Swiss trucks climb the precipitous trails of the Andes, and Swiss generators supply power in India and Yugoslavia. Swiss factories also make armaments. In addition to furnishing weapons for their own army, the Swiss manufactured antiaircraft guns, ammunition, submarine equipment and other military hardware for several major combatants in World War II. Today, Swiss manufacturers sell mines, antiaircraft rockets and other war matériel to NATO countries, mainly through sister companies in the Netherlands and Britain.

Engineering changed watchmaking from the cottage industry it primarily had been since French Protestant refugees introduced the craft into Geneva in the 16th Century and made it into big business. Today watchmaking is Switzerland's third-largest and most famous export industry. There are 2,700 factories spread over the Jura Mountains from Geneva to Schaffhausen, more than three quarters of them engaged in making parts—dials, springs and cases—and 500 in making whole watches. An annual output of nearly 45 million timepieces makes Switzerland the world's largest watch producer. Ninety-seven per cent of these timepieces are exported, mostly to the United States, West Germany and Hong Kong, which ships them all over Asia.

ALTHOUGH no country can match Switzerland's quality watches, Russia and Japan are invading the medium- and lower-price market. For this reason Swiss watchmakers have begun to diversify. Among the new products are high-precision timing devices which are used in American satellites, and in Neuchâtel the Laboratoire Suisse de Recherches Horlogères has produced a super-precise clock which, the laboratory claims, is accurate to the point of 0.3 millionth of a second per year.

Switzerland's second-largest export industry, chemicals, is, like engineering, a child of textiles. In the last decades of the 18th Century, when French émigré silk ribbon manufacturers in Basel could no longer import their aniline dyes from Revolutionary France, they began to manufacture their own. From this modest beginning grew the great chemical industry of Basel, a city which even on a clear day is covered by a cloudlike powdery haze and has a pungent odor which reaches across the border into Germany and France. From under this cloud has come one human benefaction after another. In 1941 the Geigy Company marketed DDT. CIBA develops pigments and pharmaceuticals and leads in photochemical research. Hoffmann-La Roche synthesizes vitamins, and Sandoz specializes in dyes and chemicals for textiles, paper and leather.

Related to chemistry are Switzerland's food and chocolate industries. A Swiss chemical firm,

Wander, distributes its Ovaltine all over the world. Chocolate-making, introduced by Italian *cioccolatieri*, was adapted to machine production by the Swiss. Today there are 36 chocolate factories in Switzerland, and Swiss chocolates have become known the world over for their consistently high quality, like Scotch whiskey and Bavarian beer. The Swiss themselves consume an average of 18 pounds of chocolates per person each year, one of the causes, no doubt, for the bad teeth which are a national affliction.

The best-known chocolate producer is the Nestlé Company. Beginning as a baby-food firm and expanding into a variety of processed goods, Nestlé has absorbed over the last century one competitor after another, including the old English firm of Crosse & Blackwell. Today it operates 213 factories all over the world. With sales in excess of one and a half billion dollars a year, it is the fifth-largest industrial firm in the world outside the United States. On Switzerland's economic chart, the much heralded Swiss cheese is a small item. It is near the bottom of the export list, with only about $37 million worth of shipments a year.

WHILE Swiss corporations appear rather small compared to gargantuan American companies like General Motors and Westinghouse, their size is nonetheless deceptive. Through a network of foreign subsidiaries and licensing agreements, Swiss industry spans the world. Companies like Nestlé have built plants in America and other consumer countries. Ownership, however, remains Swiss. To prevent any foreign control, some Swiss firms have adopted corporate clauses prohibiting the sale of stock to non-Swiss. Other companies allow a few foreigners to own stock, but are careful to see that a two-thirds majority of shareholders are always Swiss.

To stimulate their own commerce, the Swiss permit foreign firms to locate plants and offices in their country. The advantages of an office in Switzerland are considerable: superbly efficient banking and communications systems, a tax code favorable to foreign enterprises and, best of all, a central location for operations not only in Europe but also in the Near East and Africa. By 1964 about 700 American firms were established in Switzerland, most of them in Zurich and Geneva.

The Swiss Government controls the country's transportation lines, operates a national bank and regulates the production of arms, gunpowder and alcohol. Virtually everything else is privately owned, however, and despite the numerous welfare services provided by the Government for the people, Switzerland is a truly capitalist country. Partly because of a dedication to artisan craftsmanship, and partly because of the availability of water power all over the country, Swiss industry is decentralized. Each of 30 principal cities is industrial; so are most villages, even in such rural cantons as Glarus, Valais and Thurgau. A total of 55 firms, most of them engineering, employ more than 1,000 persons each, but most factories are small and employ fewer than 50 workers. The Swiss work week averages 46 hours. The workday begins early: at 7 a.m. Zurich is far more awake than Paris is at 10 a.m. There are almost no strikes; in a country where every worker feels he is a stockholder in the economic corporation of his land, strikes are considered unpatriotic as well as bad business.

PRODUCTION is controlled less by the Government than, after the usual fashion of European big business, by a network of producer cooperatives which reduce competition by fixing prices. The best-known cartel is that of the watchmaking industry, which sets not only prices but also quality standards. The watchmakers insist that competition among them would undermine the good reputation of Swiss watches in the world and bring disaster to the entire industry.

A counter-cooperative aimed at abolishing price controls and restoring competition was founded in 1925 by the greatest merchant in Switzerland's history, Gottlieb Duttweiler. During his lifelong battle against monopolies and high prices, Duttweiler built a chain of food-processing plants and retail stores which he expanded to encompass gasoline stations, taxi fleets, a daily newspaper and the production of motion pictures, all aimed at bringing down the cost of Swiss life and increasing its enjoyment. In 1941 Duttweiler gave a business empire worth four million dollars to his 120,-000 registered customers in the form of shares. By the time of his death in 1962, this vast cooperative included 17 factories, 413 retail stores, 136 mobile truck outlets and a bank. Cursed as a dictator by his enemies, Duttweiler is revered as a messiah by Switzerland's working people, who call him "Dutti."

AN industrial economy based on commerce with other countries is usually healthy only if it maintains a favorable balance of trade, its exports exceeding, or at least equaling, its imports. A glance at the import-export figures would seem, surprisingly, to indicate that Switzerland's economy is in serious trouble. Swiss exports have exceeded imports only three times in the last 72 years. Since 1953 Switzerland's trade balance has been continuously negative. In 1962, for instance, Swiss imports totaled slightly more than four billion dollars and exports only $2.2 billion.

But import and export figures do not tell the complete story. Switzerland's ledger is more or less balanced by "invisible exports"—sources of income which are not attributable to the movement of goods but which, in characteristic Swiss fashion, come from services. Heading these invisible exports is tourism, which brings almost half a billion dollars a year into Switzerland. Other sources of revenue are banking, insurance and transportation.

To a people who make thrift a national virtue, banking is endemic. High finance is a Protestant art, and Swiss finance was stimulated, like the textile industry, by Huguenots who fled France after the revocation of the Edict of Nantes in 1685. Though there have been French-descended bankers in Geneva for almost 300 years, Switzerland's banking system

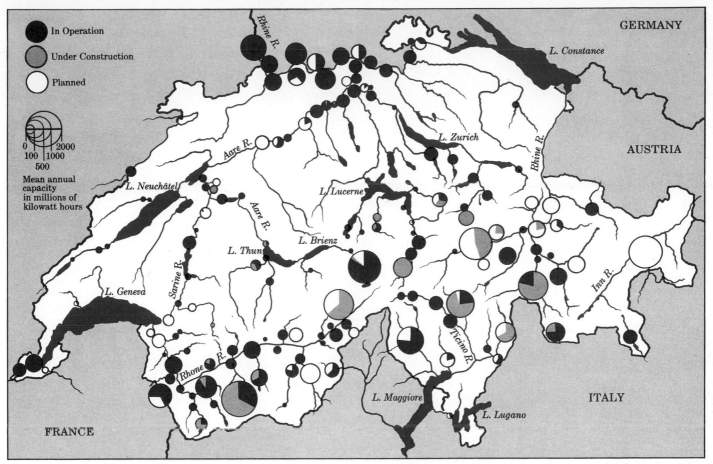

KEY TO SWISS INDUSTRY is the country's intensive hydro-electric development, shown in a map of present and projected (as of 1960) power-generating stations. The size of each circle indicates the annual kilowatt capacity of a particular power complex. Some stations near the borders are partly foreign-owned, and send a portion of their output to other countries.

flowered in the mid-19th Century with the rise of industry and commerce and the resulting boom in capital. It is no accident that the Parliament square in Bern is bordered on one side by the Parliament building and on its other three sides by banks.

Switzerland has more than 500 banks with a total of about 4,000 offices—roughly a banking establishment for every 1,400 persons. These include the Swiss National Bank, five large commercial banks, 28 state-owned cantonal banks and some 57 family-owned private banks. The number of savings accounts alone exceeds Switzerland's population. That they are the most solid banks in the world was dramatically demonstrated in July 1962 when the Swiss National Bank and the Bank for International Settlements arranged a swap of francs for $200 million with the Federal Reserve Bank of New York to bolster the American dollar. During that same year millions of francs were lent to the Government of Denmark and to banks and companies in the United States, England and Germany.

A Swiss banker, it has been said, is born, not made. He must have "the ability to observe, cool appraisal, and distinguished bearing at all times." Such a priestly description is not inappropriate to a Swiss bank, where the hushed atmosphere is more churchlike than commercial. In the great marble temples of finance which line Zurich's Bahnhofstrasse, voices never rise above a murmur, the carpets in the directors' offices are deep and soft, and the walls are covered with oil paintings. In bank windows, behind the red geranium-filled window boxes, showcases looking much like religious reliquaries glow with gold coins and colorful foreign banknotes. But the charm of these fiscal sanctuaries to depositors is not only that they are solid, but that they are also secret.

Switzerland's sympathy for all money, even that which is more or less hot, has brought a continuing flow of cash into the land. A depositor in a Swiss bank can arrange to have his account identified by number and the number known only to himself and a handful of top bank officials. Since any bank employee, should he violate a confidence, is by law subject to a 20,000-franc fine and six months' imprisonment, there is little danger of betrayal.

Much of the fugitive capital is entrusted to the private banks, which make a specialty of "discreet account management." Wealthy French have habitually stashed their fortunes in Geneva's private banks, and European and South American dictators have hidden their ill-gotten funds in Zurich. Recent depositors include ousted Cuban capitalists and Katanga Province's ex-President Moise Tshombe. Probably about 75 per cent of all business done in these private banks is for foreign accounts, and though business statements are not available, a leading private banker estimates that clandestine foreign fortunes buried in the vaults of Switzerland's private banks total considerably more than 12 billion francs, or about three billion dollars.

These hidden riches have raised Switzerland's holdings of pure gold to about $460 per capita —the figure fluctuates slightly—which is five times the per capita rate represented by the U.S. gold reserve. With every 100 Swiss franc note covered by 135 francs' worth of gold reserve, it is easy to see how the Swiss franc is the world's strongest currency.

BECAUSE of Swiss banking secrecy, nobody knows exactly how many dollars' worth of foreign dividends and interest Swiss banks bring into Switzerland each year, but it runs to many millions. Less important than banking among the invisible exports, but still highly profitable, is the related field of insurance, which brings in almost three quarters of a billion dollars in foreign premiums annually and nets, after losses have been paid, about $25

million. Insurance is a Swiss-German specialty. Based on a pragmatic calculation of probabilities, Swiss insurance can be said to have been born of Swiss mathematics. Insurance oriented, each Swiss has more than one life insurance policy and pays an average of $145 in annual life insurance premiums.

But domestic insurance makes up only part of the business done by the country's 66 private insurance companies. The major share of their premiums comes from other countries, and a large proportion of these is received by a characteristically Swiss type of firm dealing in the reinsurance of the large risks of international insurance companies. The best known, the Swiss Reinsurance Company of Zurich, has assets totaling $600 million and does 95 per cent of its business in 120 countries outside of Switzerland. It won its reputation for integrity in 1906, when it promptly paid almost two million dollars' worth of claims for losses in the San Francisco earthquake. Other disasters which it covered in part were the American hurricanes Carol in 1954 and Carla in 1961, the sunken ocean liner *Andrea Doria* in 1956 and the Los Angeles brush fires in 1961. Recently it assumed a $1.5 million share of the insurance on the new French liner, the *France*.

FOLLOWING banking among Switzerland's invisible exports is transportation. Largely dependent for survival on importing and exporting, and possessing some of the most strategic crossroads in Europe, the Swiss are the most masterly movers of goods and people in Europe. The Swiss Federal Railway, the densest and most superbly engineered in the world, is, along with Holland's, one of two state-operated railways that show a profit. More than one tenth of Switzerland's population takes a train each day, and more than 208 trains pass daily through the Gotthard tunnel.

Similarly, Switzerland's Swissair is one of the few national airlines in the world soaring on its own wings. Offering luxury and comfort unsurpassed by any other airline company, Swissair has shown an uninterrupted profit for more than 12 years. One reason is that Swiss businessmen, who are chronic travelers, are partial to their own airline. It connects their landlocked nation with 41 other countries.

In few other countries has prosperity reached quite the hyperactive peak it has in Switzerland. Unemployment is nonexistent and salaries are 50 per cent higher than they were in 1953. Savings deposits stand at $970 per citizen. Exports in 1962 rose nine per cent, and economic growth was bounding way ahead of the target rate of 4.3 per cent established by the Organization for Economic Cooperation and Development, an international economic advisory body. Investments rose in value a startling 25 per cent in 1961. Internal reserves bulge and foreign assets are double foreign liabilities. Switzerland's fiscal household, with its annual surplus in the federal budget, is something about which the Presidents of America must sweetly dream.

YET Swiss economists are worried. Despite the profits being made by everyone, the invisible exports since 1961 have not quite balanced Switzerland's trade ledger. The deficit seems to be the result of a vicious production-consumption circle created by the boom itself.

In order to manufacture its increasing quantities of goods, Switzerland has had to import more and more foreign workers. In 1963 there were more than 750,000 non-Swiss workers— a third of the entire labor force—holding jobs in Switzerland, largely from economically depressed southern Italy. Swiss hotels are recruiting their workers from as far afield as Greece and Spain. In foods and textiles, foreign workers run as high as 40 per cent, and in recent years even the chauvinist watch industry has begun hiring Italians. To reach this new clientele, newspapers run foreign-language advertisements and theaters show films in Italian.

Trouble arises when these foreign workers, called *Gastarbeiter,* or guest workers, send a portion of their salaries to support relatives at home. Such money is lost to the Swiss economy. More worrisome to the economists is the possibility that, with an increase in European prosperity, these workers may suddenly find that they can get good jobs at home and depart, leaving Swiss industry crippled.

Another problem is real-estate inflation. With expansion nearly impossible in a small and overcrowded country, real-estate values have soared alarmingly. Land in such cantons as Zurich is 10 times as expensive as it was in 1950, and building costs in 1963 were 50 per cent higher than they were 10 years earlier. Switzerland has a new generation of millionaires who made their fortunes in real-estate speculation.

Aware that their boom might very well sweep them into chaos, Swiss managers have voluntarily begun to curb the sorcerer's apprentice. Industry is freezing the hiring of foreign workers and slowing down its expansion projects. Manufacturers and wholesalers are attempting to fix produce prices. Cantonal and municipal administrations are reducing nonproductive expenditures such as hospital and school construction. In order to discourage foreign depositors, banks have discontinued interest payments on short-term deposits and have begun to charge deposit fees. Investments for expansion have been deliberately retarded, and foreign money already in Swiss banks is being held stagnant to keep it from firing the boom, from necessitating the hiring of more foreign workers and accelerating the upward spiral of prices and wages. A Swiss bank director said, "Otherwise we will be in danger of pricing ourselves right out of the world market. The Swiss franc is still strong. Very strong. And for a long time we have nothing to fear. But no currency, not even the world's strongest, can stand our kind of expansion over a long period of time."

NOT many countries would so coolly and methodically set out to inhibit their own economic growth. But the traditionally cautious Swiss are no longer interested in growth for its own sake. To the rest of the world, for which Switzerland is an economic barometer, this is reassuring. A country that perceives and then anticipates its difficulties so far in advance has a good chance of conquering them.

AIRY CAFETERIA is one of the benefits which CIBA gives to its workers. The company also provides company housing, sports facilities, hobby workshops and a well-stocked library.

ADVANCED RESEARCH absorbs two technicians at the Society of Chemical Industry in Basel, a pharmaceutical house. Its trade name, CIBA, is formed by initial letters in its title.

SPACIOUS GROUNDS surround the CIBA factory in Basel, which comprises some 200 buildings. The 54 companies CIBA owns in 20 lands employ 25,000 workers, 8,500 in Switzerland.

Skillful Technicians
to the World

Half of the Swiss labor force is engaged in industry and manual trades. In other industrialized nations, the assembly line threatens to turn workers into a breed of mindless automatons. Fortunately, Swiss manufacturing is for the most part based on advanced technology, and the skillful attention and intelligent approach required by technical industries give employees a reason for taking pride in their work. Not only the chemical and watchmaking enterprises but also those firms engaged in metalworking and textiles demand from all their technicians an exacting performance of tasks, from the initial research to the assembling process to the ultimate testing for quality.

INTRICATE ARRAY of chemical equipment is adjusted by two CIBA technicians. One of the 20 large Swiss chemical companies, CIBA exports more than 90 per cent of its products.

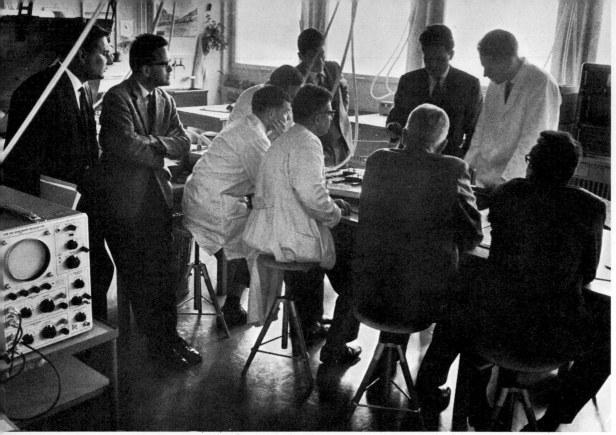

CLOSE-KNIT TEACHING STAFF at the Swiss Federal Institute of Technology observes as a departmental chairman, Professor E. Gerecke, discusses problems of computer circuits.

YOUNG INSTRUCTOR at the Institute of Technology inspects the adjustment of a spectroscope *(opposite)* which is used in connection with the analysis of chemical structures.

NEWSPAPER READING ROOM serves as a meeting place for Institute scholars. Among the Institute's alumni are Wilhelm Röntgen, the discoverer of the X-ray, and Albert Einstein.

WATER POWER is the principal source of energy in an industrialized nation with few natural resources

UNDERGROUND NERVE CENTER controls the generator-transformer units at a subterranean power station in the Grande Dixence hydroelectric development.

ARTIFICIAL LAKE created by the Grande Dixence dam stores enough water to continue producing electricity during months when the Alpine rivers are frozen over.

RELAY STATION *(opposite)* serves as a power distribution point outside the city of Lucerne, from which the electricity will be sent on to other industrial centers.

ABSOLUTE PRECISION in assembling delicate mechanisms is the hallmark of watchmaking

ULTRASONIC MACHINES at the Omega watch factory in Bienne subject each component to a bathing process. The liquid in which the parts are immersed vibrates at 20,000 oscillations per second.

FINAL ASSEMBLY of Omega watches occurs *(left)* as workers put together the various components. At a testing machine by the window an inspector measures the ticks per minute of each watch.

METICULOUS WORK is involved in oiling the minute parts of a watch *(opposite)* at the Omega watch factory. Here, 18-year-old Jacqueline Ducrez applies a drop of oil which costs $2,000 per gallon.

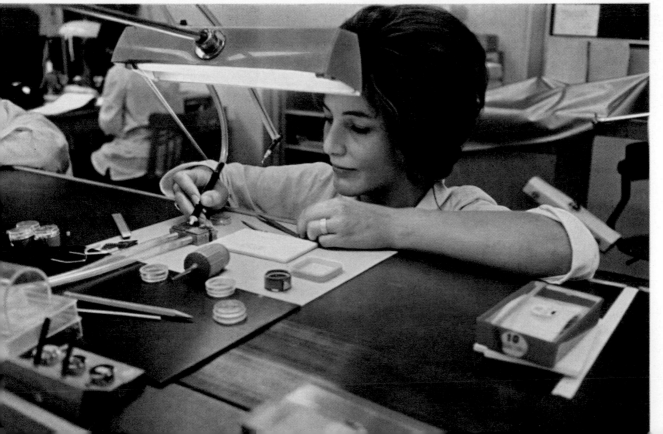

INTENT APPRENTICE hammers a piece of iron in Zurich's Oerlikon Machine Tool Works. In order to train skilled workers, Oerlikon pays apprentices a nominal salary during two to four years of study. The company instructs 150 trainees at a time.

MASTER WATCHMAKER Jean Friedli *(foreground, opposite)*, chief of an Omega assembly track, concentrates on a minute watch part. Omega employs 3,600 workers in its Bienne plant, 500 more abroad. Yearly output is about a million watches.

ARMAMENT PRODUCTION at Oerlikon proceeds *(right)* as a worker tools a gun barrel on a lathe. Metal-processing firms like Oerlikon not only make weapons but also produce diesel engines, agricultural machines and industrial equipment.

Military policemen direct Army traffic near Andermatt, a town with an arsenal and a mountainside fortress that guard the strategic

The Government's Orderly Pace

4

St. Gotthard Pass. Switzerland maintains no standing army, but members of its reserve forces maneuver for several weeks each year.

THE square in Glarus on the first Sunday in May looks like a combination of Wagner's opera *Die Meistersinger* and a Madison Square Garden prizefight. Crowds mill about, bands blare and houses are festooned with flowers and bunting. From windows and doors flutter the red flags of Switzerland, with their white crosses, and the red flags of the canton, on which are depicted Glarus' patron saint, Saint Fridolin. The festival atmosphere is misleading, however. The tourists who have been jamming the highways leading to Glarus since 8:00 a.m. are coming not for a pagan spring rite but with the solemn purpose of watching primitive Swiss democracy in action. They come to see the Landsgemeinde, traditional plenary gathering of the people of Glarus since 1387, convene for its yearly meeting.

At 9 o'clock churchbells start ringing. From the Rathaus (city hall) a brass band playing the national anthem leads a procession which includes 84 members of the legislative Landrat, 26 judges and seven cantonal councilors toward the open square where the meeting will take place. The seven councilors wear cutaway coats, striped trousers, top hats and carnation boutonnieres. These dignitaries are followed by a platoon of soldiers in field-gray uniforms. The procession moves down Glarus' main street, turns right at the schoolhouse and enters the Landsgemeindeplatz.

FOR Americans, the scene in the square is familiar from photographs in schoolbooks. Six thousand men are sitting on row after row of wooden benches which surround a small elevated platform with a speaker's podium, loudspeakers and a table at which two court stenographers are waiting. The front seats are filled with young men from 12 to 20 years of age who have come for their annual lesson in democracy. The rest are taken by the voters, men of the canton of Glarus, 20 years old and older. Women do not have the vote. Tourists watch with the women and children from rooftops and from the geranium- and petunia-garlanded windows of the high-gabled houses. Except for a few wisps of cloud clinging to the Vorderglärnisch, the 7,646-foot-high mountain which towers over the square, the heavens are blue. In Glarus, where it rains a lot, the weather on this Sunday has been fair for 30 years.

In a recent year, the Landammann, or cantonal President, a strong, stocky six-footer named Hermann Feusi, declared the Landsgemeinde open at 9:30 a.m. The Vice President, Fritz Stucki, also wearing a cutaway, read the Constitutional oath, and the 6,000 voters raised their right hands in allegiance. The preliminaries were followed by the election by acclamation of local government officials. Then the President moved on to the 151-page agenda containing 21 legislative proposals which the citizens of Glarus had been studying and arguing over for two weeks.

The most controversial item on the agenda was the Sunday opening of shops during the Christmas season. Landammann Feusi explained that shopkeepers were behind the proposal and labor unions were against it. He recognized the waving hand of Hans Freuler, a store clerk from the village of Ennenda, who said, "The five-day week has been accepted all over Switzerland. Farmers have time to make their purchases on Saturdays, especially in winter." A shop clerk from Näfels, Josef Gunsch, said, "We need a rest like everyone else," and was loudly applauded. The next speaker, a shopkeeper from Bilten named David Stüssi, said, "If we close our shops on Sundays our farmers will do their Christmas shopping in Lucerne and Zurich." He was booed; there were cheers for the next speaker, Father Ulrich Jost, Roman Catholic priest from Linthal, who said, "Sundays and Christmas belong to God and not to the shopkeepers of Glarus."

That seemed to settle it. A showing of hands produced a massive majority for the continued Sunday closing of all shops in the canton. The Landsgemeinde moved on to matters of taxation, old-age insurance, animal protection and hunting and the cantonal budget. By 1:15 p.m. all 21 articles had been debated and voted upon and Landammann Feusi closed the meeting. The men dispersed into the town's *Wirtschaften*— taverns and inns—for food and drink, and then met again at the annual Glarus fair. All afternoon and evening there was debating over beer and wine. There was no dancing, however. The Landsgemeinde is a serious, male affair with no place for frivolities.

SUCH popular assemblies, once the custom in all central Switzerland, still exist as the official governing bodies of three of the 25 cantons. Their spirit is less that of a philosophical discussion than of a conclave of armed warriors proclaiming their individual liberties. In Appenzell, even today, the voters carry swords as a symbol of their status as free men with a right to vote and bear arms. These assemblies still reflect the spirit of the Rütli "oath comradeship" with which the Everlasting League was formed in 1291, and their origin is found in the fierce passion for liberty of the ancient Germanic tribes.

In cantons where there is no Landsgemeinde, the political processes are no less democratic. In the canton of Zurich, most thickly populated, with 952,304 inhabitants, voters elect not only the legislature but also the cantonal council, judges and even schoolteachers. The people themselves have the power to initiate new legislation, and all proposed laws are subject to popular referendum. So busy is the political life that voters go to the polls as often as 10 times a year.

The Swiss citizen's position is that he is his own master and government is merely a servant. He dislikes all authority on principle and is ever ready to combat it. But as much as he hates authority he loves order, and he recognizes that to sustain the order he loves a certain amount of authority is necessary. So he accepts government as an unavoidable evil while never quite forgiving it for being there.

THIS vacillation between love for freedom and love for order is the clue to Swiss political life. Few people in the world know their national history as well as the Swiss. Every citizen feels he and his countrymen *are* the state, and this common feeling is the Confederation's strength. A Swiss clings stubbornly and anxiously to his traditions. His mentality is too conservative, too deeply rooted in the nation's past for him to experiment in political excesses. When the Swiss voters go to the polls to tell the authorities what to do, they are almost invariably more conservative than the authorities. The country's seven national political parties, although they range from a group called the Catholic Conservatives to another called the Socialists, are all equally moderate in most respects. In a country where it is impossible to divide the population into nonowning workers and nonworking owners, Marxism has never succeeded in making much headway.

Swiss government operates not from the top down but from the bottom up. The Swiss is a citizen, first of all, of his commune, a unit small enough for the exercise of direct democracy.

Because he has a direct voice in making the laws which govern him, the average Swiss citizen is probably more interested in, and knowledgeable about, local and national issues than the citizens of any other country.

A Swiss is also a citizen of his canton, which, compared with most U.S. states, is also a small and manageable political unit. The cantons govern in a middle area, wielding authority in matters that extend beyond the geographical domains of their member communes but giving up their sovereignty in turn in national matters to the federal Government in Bern.

THIS system based on cooperation—of the people with each other within the communes, of the communes within the cantons and the cantons within the Confederation—is far from a natural thing for such an aggregation of different cultures, languages and religions. The present functioning state took centuries to mature, and it results from a common determination of the people to tolerate one another and live together, if not exactly in sympathy and love, at least in peace. Essentially it is made possible by the spirit of compromise, by the idea of neutrality which is so deeply bred into the blood and bones of a Swiss.

Bred into the blood and bones as well is something that perhaps can best be called an instinct for democratic self-government. The Swiss have governed themselves for almost seven centuries, although for hundreds of years they paid token fealty to emperors and kings. Over these centuries they have acquired that curiously ambivalent and even contradictory frame of mind necessary for democratic man, that frame of mind which allows a man to cooperate for the common good even while he passionately objects to half of what his government and his fellow citizens are doing. It is an ability to make haste slowly, so to speak, guarding what is good and useful from the past while remaining flexible enough to make changes when and where change is demanded.

This instinct for flexible but stable self-rule is presumably difficult to acquire, to judge by the history of the many countries that have tried democracy and failed to make it work. Only the people of Britain and the United States seem to possess the instinct in the same degree as the Swiss. Professor Erich Kahler says that Switzerland is the only country besides the United States "in which democracy is the sole substratum of life, in which all specific forms of life derive from democracy, in which nation and democracy are synonymous."

A comparison between Switzerland and the United States is hardly surprising in view of the fact that an exchange of ideas between the two countries entered into both of their constitutions. The concepts of Swiss philosophers had a profound influence on American political thought and on the men who framed the Declaration of Independence. In turn, the U.S. Constitution influenced the Swiss Constitution of 1848. In part because of this mutual exchange, the largest republic in the world and the oldest adopted comparable federal forms of government which allowed their states a large measure of sovereignty.

The most striking similarity between the two federations is their use of a bicameral legislative system. The Swiss Federal Assembly, like the Congress of the United States, has a Senate, called the Ständerat, or Council of States, and a House of Representatives, called the Nationalrat, or National Council. In the Council of States each canton has two members, no matter what its size. In the National Council the people are represented in proportion to the number of electors in each canton. Thus Zurich has 35 deputies to the National Council and Uri only one. For a bill to become law it must, as in America, be passed by a majority of the members of both chambers.

There are, however, more differences than similarities between the structures of the U.S. and Swiss governments. The most obvious difference between the two is in their executive branches. Partly because of their innate distrust of authority, the Swiss could never tolerate a single head of government like the American president or the British prime minister. The Swiss, who have seen so many dictators rise to power in neighboring countries, instinctively feel that a single leader is potentially dangerous. This is one of the reasons, no doubt, that Swiss statesmen are rarely striking personalities. A spectacular man would get short shrift in Bern. Switzerland has no leaders other than men with a pious devotion to responsibility and to duty.

The executive branch of the Swiss Government is the Federal Council, made up of seven men elected by the two houses of Parliament meeting in joint session. Geography, language, religion and political party are considerations in the make-up of the Council, which is supposed to be as representative as possible of all of Switzerland. There can be no more than one councilor from a canton and, by custom, the three large city cantons of Zurich, Bern and Vaud (Lausanne) have permanent representation.

The Federal Council fulfills the functions of both a president and his cabinet. As in the U.S. Cabinet, each of the members is in charge of a branch of the federal Government—the Political Department which handles foreign affairs, the Department of the Interior, the Department of Public Economy and so on. The Council has

---

THE PERVASIVE CIVIL SERVICE

As in most modern democracies, the work of actually administering Switzerland is carried out not by elected officials but by a large group of appointed, professional civil servants. Switzerland has, in fact, two types of civil service employees, those appointed by the cantons and those who work for the federal Government. The federal rolls numbered 110,884 employees in 1962. A large proportion of these—over 72 per cent—were employed in operating the Government-controlled telephone, telegraph and railroad services, but the remainder, more than 30,000, were engaged in running various Government departments such as foreign affairs and finance. As the federal Government takes on more and more of the administrative duties that the cantons, in modern, industrialized Switzerland, are unable to handle, the federal civil service will undoubtedly grow still larger, and some Swiss fear that this will result in increased red tape as well as bureaucratic interference in the legislative process.

a great measure of autonomy. It is not directly responsible to the legislature for its actions, and the Council does not lose office (as would the Cabinet in Britain) just because one of its policies has been defeated in the legislature. In fact, councilors generally have their jobs for life if they wish to serve, although some resign after two or three terms to return to private life.

A chief function of this close-knit, seven-man executive is conciliation and coordination. Leaders of the parties in the legislature often consult the Council when they wish to propose new legislation. The Council decides whether the proposed law would be beneficial or, if several groups have presented similar proposals, if a compromise bill can be worked out. The Council then, as often as not, drafts the bill on which the legislature will vote. In practice, such is the Swiss passion for cooperation, this advisory role gives the Council considerable power.

THE president of Switzerland is chairman of the Council. He is elected for one year by the legislature, but the election is a formality, since by a system of rotation the former vice president becomes the president and the new vice president is next on the list. Ludwig von Moos, who succeeded Willy Spühler as President on January 1, 1964, is leader of the Catholic Conservative Party and has been a member of the Federal Council since 1959. As President he conducts the meetings of the Council and performs all the functions of a head of state, but he also retains his former post as Minister of Justice and Police. His salary is the same as that of his fellow councilors—about $17,500 a year. As the French historian André Siegfried noted of a past president, "The Swiss like to see him arrive at his office early in the morning by some democratic form of conveyance such as the tramway, and stay there until evening."

The most remarkable feature of the Swiss system is the provision for the people to intervene directly in the national legislative process. The Constitution states that, with very few exceptions, no bill passed by the Federal Assembly shall become law for 90 days. During that period any Swiss citizen who collects 30,000 signatures can, by his right of referendum, force the Government to submit the disputed legislation to a popular vote. By his right of initiative, a Swiss with the support of 50,000 fellow citizens can propose changes in the Constitution which must then be voted on by the Federal Assembly and submitted to the electorate. In addition, any Constitutional amendment originating in the legislature must be submitted to a popular vote. Initiative and referendum are remarkably effective extensions on a national scale of the individual's right of self-rule as recognized in the cantonal Landsgemeinde.

The Swiss federal Government, like that of the United States, has a third branch, the judiciary. But the Swiss Supreme Federal Tribunal is both larger and less powerful than the U.S. Supreme Court. Its 26 judges, who are elected for six-year terms by the Federal Assembly rather than appointed by the president for life (as in the United States), have no powers for testing the constitutionality of federal law. The Tribunal is, however, charged with deciding whether cantonal and federal law are in conflict and with settling legal disputes between canton and canton. In addition it is Switzerland's final court of appeals and has a general mandate from the Constitution to act as guardian of the rights of the people.

THE Supreme Federal Tribunal sits in Lausanne rather than in the capital, Bern. It has been said that in another important sense Bern is not the only center of power in Switzerland. Bern is a federal town, seat of a labyrinth of administration. A more influential though unofficial capital is Zurich. In a country which lives by commerce and industry, many important decisions and policies must inevitably come from its industrial, commercial and financial center. Zurichers are cynically aware of this; they have some of the best and most influential newspapers and send up to Bern one of the most powerful corps of lobbyists in Europe. A Zurich journalist said, "Bern may be the capital of our political democracy but Zurich is the capital of our financial oligarchy. The big cats are perfectly willing to let the little kittens run the country so long as they don't interfere too much in its business.''

The top-heavy concentration of money and power in Zurich is only one of the problems facing the Swiss Government as the result of the country's ever-increasing industrialization. Because of diminishing agriculture and the greater and greater concentration of people in the manufacturing towns, the balance between urban and rural Switzerland, which has been the Confederation's foundation, is slowly disappearing. Communes and cities are growing beyond their ancient boundaries and merging with neighboring communities. Cantons are coalescing into large economic units while mountain valleys are being abandoned. Today only a quarter of all Swiss live in the communes of which they are citizens. Of the 3,095 communes, almost half have grown smaller in the last 100 years while the total population of the country has more than doubled. Switzerland's population of 5.8 million will probably double again by the year 2050. Since the greater part of this new population can be expected to settle in the existing urban centers of Zurich, Basel, Bern, Geneva and Lausanne, the imbalance between a few enormous metropolitan areas and a semideserted rural hinterland will become more and more marked. The big population concentrations will inevitably undermine communal and cantonal sovereignty and strengthen the central Government.

ALREADY the strain is beginning to show. Sometimes federal laws left to the cantons for execution are ignored. The Zermatt typhoid scandal of 1963 was an example of this. Federal laws provide for the purification of water and sewage disposal, but leave their administration to the cantons. In Zermatt, the local officials had failed to enlarge and improve the sewage disposal system although the town, a preserve of well-to-do Alpinists and skiers, was expanding fast. When an old and inadequate

sewer pipe gave way, the town fathers did nothing about it. As a result, the town's water supply was contaminated, approximately 400 people contracted typhoid fever and at least four died.

A second example has been the shocking neglect of Switzerland's lakes and rivers. Because of local disregard for federal regulations, many of Switzerland's famous lakes have become perils to health. Doctors have warned that swimmers may contract skin eczema, typhoid fever and even poliomyelitis in the waters of Lake Constance and the lakes of Geneva, Neuchâtel and Zurich. According to the Federal Bureau of Lakes and Waterways, only a few mountain lakes are still clean and in most others, fish are becoming extinct.

LOCAL inertia is likely to draw Bern deeper and deeper into the business of government as time goes on. Slowly the Swiss are being forced to realize that the problems of the future may be beyond the capacity of communes and cantons to resolve. Just as in the United States, where the Depression, two world wars and the rise of technology have multiplied the functions of the Government in Washington, so similar forces are presently enlarging the size and duties of the administrative offices in Bern.

For a tradition-bound people who have grown accustomed to looking backward instead of forward, adaptation to new and more complicated forms of cooperation will not be easy. Love of tradition is a stabilizing virtue, but in a live democracy another instinct is needed: a capacity of each generation to solve its new problems and to bequeath a healthy state to the next generation. More and more the 20th Century will demand modifications of Switzerland's seven-century-old concepts. There are signs that the Swiss are learning: in 1963 the voters elected to leave the final decision on whether to acquire nuclear arms to Bern, thereby in this one instance relinquishing, in a very un-Swiss fashion, their right to have the last word themselves.

The National Council, the chamber of the Swiss legislature comparable to the U.S. House of Representatives, conducts a meeting in Bern.

Restrictions Which Are Calculated to Liberate

Realizing that only by regimenting part of their lives can they maintain genuine independence, the Swiss perform their social responsibilities with assiduity. True democracy in any area larger than a small community can be both time-consuming and inefficient, but the Swiss would rather take the time and trouble than surrender a single right. In those few cantons which still have the Landsgemeinde, or open-air citizens' meeting, a popular assembly made up of all eligible males wields the local legislative power; in effect, the electorate is sovereign. Another form of service to the state is the compulsory military draft. By participating in ruling and defending the nation, the Swiss people stay unusually close to their Government.

PREPAREDNESS is maintained by involving the entire citizenry in military defense

FORTIFICATION, a well-maintained tank trap *(right)* constructed in World War II to guard the Sarnen Valley from attacks, is fenced off from a family raking hay.

TOUR OF DUTY during a 20-day period each year provides training for reservists *(opposite).* The soldiers are being inspected at a temporary installation in Wolhusen.

YOUNG MARKSMEN compete for prizes *(below)* in the Boys' Shooting Competition held every September at the Albisgütli, a mountain slope outside Zurich.

meetings once a year

TAKING AN OATH, newly elected judges raise three fingers, signifying Switzerland's three original cantons, during the annual Landsgemeinde at Sarnen, the capital of Obwalden canton.

ADDRESSING THE ELECTORATE, Hans Gasser, the outgoing President, or Landammann, of Obwalden, speaks to the male assembly *(left)*. The first Landsgemeinde met in Glarus in 1387.

LINING THE WALL, electors listen to a speech delivered during the Landsgemeinde at Sarnen. The meeting is held each May on the Landenberg, a hill above the small town of Sarnen.

5

Inner Turmoil beneath an Outward Calm

MEN may rule Switzerland, but we as women rule the men, so we *really* rule Switzerland," says Frau Hanna Seiler. "We make the men get for us what we want. If we wish a law passed in Parliament, they do it for us." Her friend, Frau Ida Monn, says, "Swiss women have all freedoms, all liberties. We are the happiest women in Europe, perhaps in the world."

The ladies are officers of one of the strangest of Switzerland's multitude of organizations, *Der Bund der Schweizerinnen gegen das Frauenstimmrecht*, which translated means the Society of Swiss Women against the Right to Vote. Frau Seiler, the dark-haired, energetic wife of a

rural Swiss physician, is the mother of three grown sons and a daughter and is an authority on English literature. Frau Monn, a handsome blonde woman, is the wife of a Lucerne banker and the mother of four daughters. The two women spend much of their time successfully persuading Swiss women that it would be a disaster if they shared the men's right to vote. "The State is the affair of men," says Frau Monn. "Voting women would be a catastrophe for our terribly male Constitution. The balance of power would be destroyed."

"Swiss women like strong, male men," says Frau Seiler. "Every Swiss woman is a little Eve, intuitively sensing that a man must rule, that political responsibility makes men more manly. We are far happier in our role of queens. Like the queen of the bees we rule our hives. We are not afraid. It can never come to pass that women will vote in Switzerland."

The question of women's vote is sporadically argued in the federal Parliament. Hans Düby of the Socialist Party, who is a member of the National Council, has said, "Women are Swiss citizens as well as men, and it is illegal to exclude them." But National Councilor Paul Burgdorfer of the more conservative Farmers' Party answers, "I have frequently discussed the problem with my wife and she is against the women's vote." Swiss playwright Friedrich Dürrenmatt, who lives in Neuchâtel, one of three cantons (along with Vaud and Geneva) which have given women the franchise in cantonal elections, believes it will be another 30 years before women will be allowed at the national polls. He says, "Unfortunately the women who want to vote are mild, timid, workers' wives. Those against it are devastatingly influential matriarchs who run the country without the vote."

Switzerland has, without doubt, its share of devastatingly influential matriarchs. Perhaps there is a warning from history in a statue overlooking the Limmat River in Zurich. It portrays some armored women of the Middle Ages who, by gathering up spears and swords, so frightened an approaching Austrian army that Zurich was saved from attack. Looking at this statue, one is reminded that power in Switzerland has never been exclusively in male hands.

LIKE almost everything in Switzerland, the relationship between the sexes is a kind of armed truce in which hostilities are circumvented by a spirit of neutrality. Home is the woman's duchy; as guardian of the hearth, she is the very center of Swiss life. A man has his civic responsibilities, his seemingly endless elections and his annual military duty, and he has his social life with a variety of clubs, weekly card games with friends in cafés, and choral

societies, in which women have little or no part.

A Swiss woman, especially in the German-speaking part of Switzerland, tends to look on such pastimes as frivolous wastes of time and money. Her idea of a worthwhile expenditure is the purchase of the latest model vacuum cleaner. Her mania for cleaning, for seeking out invisible particles of dust, is an obsession over which psychiatrists have pondered. An American professor who lived in Zurich was driven almost mad by women beating rugs every morning in the courtyard of his apartment house.

A WOMAN'S rewards for dedication and hard work are pride in her house and in her family. Swiss families are often large, and children are brought up strictly. Their good manners and evident happiness reflect the security and confidence that well-managed homes can give. A Swiss's strong sense of family is not limited to his immediate household. It extends to vast numbers of cousins, some of them in remote country villages. Strong family pride is responsible for a wide interest in heraldry. Almost every Swiss family boasts an armorial crest which is worn by the men on signet rings.

To help them to wage their low-keyed war between the sexes, Swiss women have mobilized in another organization, the formidable *Bund Schweizerischer Frauenvereine* (Union of Swiss Women's Clubs), through which they exercise a guardianship over public morals. The *Frauenverein,* according to its national secretary, Fräulein Henriette Cartier, is not to be confused with an American women's club. "We don't spend our afternoons playing bridge, drinking tea or organizing raffles," she says. "Our aims are purely professional and sociological—we encompass all the problems of women. Of course we strive for the women's vote. But even without it we are not doing too badly."

Adhering to the puritan premise that the male is base and sinful and the female is a guiding angel, the Society ladies challenge the men where it hurts—through their wine and women. Swiss men like their beer and *Kirschwasser;* next to the French and Italians they are the heaviest drinkers in Europe. So the *Frauenverein* has gone after the public houses, forcing a midnight curfew in Zurich which brings the city's night life to an abrupt and frustrating closing when it seems only to have begun. Having succeeded so well, the *Frauenverein* wisely seeks to avoid the limelight and the curses of thirsty Zurichers. "Of course the authorities consulted us," says Fräulein Cartier, "but it was the *men* of Zurich who voted the early closing. The Zuricher is a puritan who rises early and goes to bed early."

The *Frauenverein* ladies have also attempted to curb the Swiss taste for alcohol by setting up their own *alkoholfreie* establishments. In Zurich, 18 restaurants and three hotels fall into this alcohol-free category. Since the *alkoholfreie* restaurants serve inexpensive food, their clientele is large, and they boast many converts to such *Frauenverein* specialties as nonalcoholic beer and unfermented grape juice. In 1962 the Society's establishments served 150,000 gallons of milk and 30,000 gallons of sweet cider.

THE ladies' temperance drive has abetted the spread of two other types of nonalcoholic establishments: vegetarian restaurants and coffee houses. Vegetarian restaurants have prospered in recent years, since many Swiss have been converted to the theories of Dr. Bircher-Benner, a raw-vegetable prophet who died in 1939 at the age of 71. Bircher-Benner's most popular concoction, called *Birchermüesli*, is a pudding made of oatmeal, fresh fruits and nuts.

Coffee houses, older and more traditional Swiss institutions, are also growing in number and popularity. There are about 350 coffee houses in Zurich alone. The most famous is the 50-year-old Odeon, an ornate Edwardian parlor on Bellevue Platz, which has marble tables, crystal chandeliers, potted rubber plants and a highbrow literary clientele. James Joyce worked and socialized there during the years he lived in Zurich, and so did Thomas Mann. Less sedate establishments, with exotic names like Java, Bali and Hollywood, appeal to the university crowd. Young Zurichers drink less alcohol than

their fathers, but they down large quantities of coffee. Good Swiss coffee is so strong and invigorating that conceivably the Swiss police are correct when they attribute more youthful delinquencies to the coffee houses than to bars.

One of the goals of the *Frauenverein* has been to increase professional opportunities for Swiss women. Today there are women taxi drivers and streetcar conductors, and over 40 per cent of the country's industrial workers are women. There are 27 *Pfarrerinnen*, women Protestant ministers, and several dozen more women are currently studying theology. Only one of these *Pfarrerinnen*, however, has been accorded the honor of a full ministry. The rest are auxiliary preachers and must content themselves with assistantships or with serving as chaplains in hospitals.

Almost every university has some female professors. At the University of Zurich, Professor Hedi Fritz-Niggli is a mineralogist and Professor Verena Meyer an atom-physicist. Professor Elisabeth Schmid teaches paleontology at Basel and Professor Kitty Ponse endocrinology at Geneva. At least three Swiss women—opera singers Lisa Della Casa and Maria Stader and actress Maria Schell—are famous outside of Switzerland.

IN the realm of illicit sex, on the other hand, the *Frauenverein* seems to be making less progress. The successful closing of night spots increased rather than discouraged the spread of prostitution, which proliferates despite volunteer "midnight missionaries"—finger-wagging ladies who roam the red-light districts preaching little sermons.

In Switzerland's characteristic spirit of fair play, the less demonstrative forms of streetwalking were given a kind of legal sanction by a Zurich court, which ruled that a woman is not guilty of soliciting just because she walks the streets alluringly made-up and clothed. If a man is attracted and introduces himself, that is his business, said the court, and the girl is not to blame. When the Federal Tribunal in Lausanne reversed the decision, judging that any display of merchandise is an offer for business, the girls did not brood over the decision —they went out and bought dogs. Dogs have to be walked and no one can arrest a lady for walking one. Some girls, discovering they loved dogs, now have two or three, and as a result, no respectable woman of Zurich finds it safe to walk a dog after dark—her husband or brother has to do it for her.

Because a respectable appearance must be kept up at any cost, a Swiss's extramarital love is managed with great decorum. If a businessman is wealthy enough to afford a mistress, he usually keeps her in another town where he does business. She, in turn, is expected to be a good Swiss citizen as well as a good Swiss mistress; she maintains her fastidious apartment with her own earnings as a secretary or a receptionist. "They write off Geneva as a city of sin," complained a Genevese, "but the Geneva weekend is a regular feature in the life of a Bernese male."

CAREFUL and prudent as they are, the Swiss are not, as they are sometimes described, a humorless people. Their broad, self-ridiculing type of humor reaches its greatest flowering in cabaret theaters. These startling manifestations of free speech were given fresh impetus by Thomas Mann's daughter, Erika, who in the early 1930s toured Switzerland with a satiric review called *The Pepper Mill* and then helped found one of Zurich's leading cabarets. Today the cabaret theaters are filled with well-wined-and-dined burghers guffawing at malicious parodies of themselves. Among the most effective cabaret comedians are the team of Walter Morath and Voli Geiler, who accuse their fellow countrymen of doing little but milking cows and tourists and who ridicule Swiss Government policy by noting that the word neutrality is first cousin to "neuter," which means "neither male nor female, neither fish nor fowl, neither hot nor warm, neither here nor there."

Such an inverted, and often rather cruel, humor may be an escape from Swiss sobriety and from a chronic inability to be happy. Geneva, with its beautiful lakefront and handsome buildings, is nonetheless a troubled city, dominated from the highest hill in the old city by Calvin's Gothic cathedral, which watches over the town like a brooding conscience. In Zurich the guardian is a dour-faced statue of Zwingli which stands outside the Wasserkirche (the "Water Church," being so named because it stands on the bank of the Limmat River). Zwingli is portrayed with a sword in one hand and a Bible in the other, the statue keeping glum vigil over the town's gayest quarter, the Altstadt.

ALTHOUGH Calvinism began in Geneva and has profoundly influenced the Swiss psyche, it made its broadest impression on the Anglo-Saxon countries of England and America. Switzerland is predominantly Zwinglian. Zwingli's preaching did not insist on the terrors of hell-fire to quite the degree Calvin's did, but his emphasis on the sinfulness of pleasure was quite sufficient for his faith to be called puritanical. Zwingli's doctrines still exert a constant pressure on Swiss life. Even non-believers have a sense of being watched, if not by a justly wrathful God then by their neighbors. Everyone is perpetually on his guard and self-righteousness is a national characteristic. A Swiss, like people from other countries with a basically puritan heritage, is always striving painstakingly to hide his own transgressions at the same time that he keeps himself thoroughly cognizant of everyone else's.

And there is no doubt that the Zwinglian creed provides additional opportunities for a certain moral duplicity. Zwinglianism is a practical, rationalistic form of Protestantism, largely unencumbered by either the judicial, closely reasoned theology or the hard and fast moral dictates of Calvinism. According to historian Erich Kahler, the Swiss "are religious in a practical, sober, common-sense fashion, just as their Zwingli, who did not bother much about theological subtleties and took over. . . just those Reformation principles which seemed to him suitable and useful for the moral standards of his people."

A lack of imperative moral rules makes it possible for a Swiss to subordinate, when necessary, his religious convictions to his pleasures. But since the average Swiss has been taught since earliest youth that any deviation from a straight path of duty and industry will bring swift and awful retribution, indulgence in the illicit stirs up a painful conflict in his mind. And with ever-increasing prosperity, the money and the opportunity to sin increase as well. Thus the modern, urban Swiss is racked by temptation (and should he stray, by guilt) far more frequently than his poor ancestor herding cows in a remote mountain valley. It is partly to still these nagging voices of temptation and guilt that a Swiss businessman works so diligently and is so scrupulously honest, if very tough and hardheaded, in his business dealings. A Swiss banker who has worked 11 years in America has said that "We Swiss are the world's most pragmatic businessmen. The toughest American businessman is a softheaded idealist compared with a Swiss. And even more than Americans, the Swiss are materialistically oriented."

A difference between Swiss materialism and the American variety is that an American makes money as a means to enjoy life, for the pleasure of possessing things, while a Swiss tends to feel that money is the end itself. He does not enjoy it; he worries and frets over it. Perhaps the most devastating attack on Swiss materialism was made by the German philosopher Hermann Keyserling. Though his book *The Spectrum of Europe* was published 35 years ago, mention of it will still drive a Swiss into a purple rage. "Even the rich Swiss live in a pinched way," wrote Keyserling. "They have no understanding at all of how to spend money."

Professor Karl Barth, a more judicious observer of the Swiss, takes a more moderate view. He says, "Neither Switzerland nor the United States has returned so completely to materialism as, say, Germany. We are all, Swiss as well as Americans and the rest, human beings with human qualities and human frailties."

Human frailties there certainly are in Switzerland. While murders and other crimes of violence are comparatively rare, the high incidence of sex crimes became a public scandal a few years ago. Social workers blamed erotic films and cheap literature for arousing sensuality in the introverted Swiss temperament. Another factor, the social workers decided, echoing their counterparts in the United States, was too much prosperity, which provides economic independence for young people under 20 years of age.

The young are not the only ones who seek release from their careful, introverted lives. It

---

ZWINGLI'S LIFE AND RELIGIOUS DOCTRINES

Ulrich Zwingli, Switzerland's great Reformation theologian, was born in 1484 in the mountain village of Wildhaus in the canton of St. Gall. At the age of 16, the young Zwingli was sent to the University of Vienna. Returning to Switzerland, he graduated from the University of Basel, and at 22 was ordained and elected parish priest of Glarus. In his 10 years in Glarus he studied Greek and Hebrew so that he could read the Bible in its original languages. He gradually became convinced that the true Christian path was to follow Christ's teachings rather than the complex rituals and doctrines of popes and prelates.

BREAK WITH THE CHURCH

After leaving Glarus, Zwingli went to Einsiedeln, where he began to preach about the Gospels and to attack such Roman Catholic customs as pilgrimages and the selling of indulgences. Moving to Zurich in 1519, he widened his attack to include fasting, saint worship, the worship of images, the celibacy of the clergy and finally the Mass itself. When the bishop of Constance admonished the people of Zurich to beware of heretical preaching, the reformer produced his famous 67 theses and ably defended his doctrines before Zurich's Great Council in 1523. The Zurichers sided with Zwingli, and thus committed themselves to an open rupture with Rome and the papacy.

A VIOLENT END

The religious division between those parts of Switzerland faithful to Rome and those following Zwingli soon flared into open warfare. In 1531 Zwingli urged an attack on the Catholics. It was the Catholic confederates, however, who attacked, and on October 11 Zwingli was killed at the disastrous battle of Kappel. His corpse was quartered and then burned. A stone marks the spot where he died. Its inscription reads in part: ". . . [he died] for the truth and freedom of the Christian Church."

will surprise no one that a people as controlled as the Swiss must escape now and then into paroxysms. Their most famous outlet is the *Basler Fastnacht*, Basel's yearly carnival, during which the city's customarily sober citizens don costumes and masks and pursue one another like satyrs for two days and two nights. Explosive Saturday nights are a usual and accepted occurrence in virtually every Swiss city, and the consumption of liquor is such that all the *Frauenverein's* efforts seem to have been in vain.

THEN there are the tragic statistics. Switzerland has the world's seventh-highest suicide rate and one of the highest incidences of mental illness in Europe. About 10 per cent of the patients in mental hospitals are alcoholics. According to the Swiss Anti-Alcoholic Secretariat, the Swiss people spend $326 million a year on alcoholic beverages, more than is spent on bread and education combined. Despite a federal law prohibiting the manufacture of absinthe, addiction to it is sometimes blamed for the high rate of lunacy among the people living in the Jura Mountains and the Alps.

Psychiatrists point out that a gloomy outlook and a disposition toward melancholia and despair are characteristic of mountain people and are just as prevalent among Austrians and Bavarians. Alpine people are high-tempered and taut-nerved, and they crack under strain more quickly, it is said, than do plains dwellers. But Switzerland also has the *Föhn*, a warm high-pressure air mass which periodically rolls down from the mountains and settles over the valleys. Under its sultry spell, blood courses wildly through veins, death notices increase in newspapers and clinics report an exaggerated unrest in patients.

For Switzerland's high suicide rate a Zurich journalist blames "the disparity between human instinct and human convention," and says, "While we are free politically, we feel socially imprisoned. Too many of us simply can't endure this." Playwright Dürrenmatt believes another cause to be the increasing leisure resulting from industrial automation. Obsessed by their mania for work, the Swiss do not know what to do with free time. Like a colony of insects when its work processes are interrupted, they are disoriented by leisure. A Bern University psychiatrist, Dr. Hans Heimann, lays the blame right on materialism. He says, "Even a minor financial setback may get a Swiss worrying his head off, upset his mental balance and in some cases lead to suicide."

One thing no Swiss can bear is feeling that he has not securely provided for his future. He has a squirrel's natural instinct for hoarding. At the first news of any world crisis, Swiss housewives lay in enormous stocks of nonperishable foods. The same instinct makes the Swiss the world's greatest investors in insurance —12 per cent of their national income. Such natural prudence is a Swiss's inheritance from his peasant mountain ancestors.

KNOWN for frugality, the Swiss nevertheless are famous also for their generosity. Psychologists attribute Swiss benevolence to a feeling of guilt arising from prosperity and uninvolvement in the world's anguished wars. A cynical Zurich businessman calls Swiss philanthropy "a mask, a pretense of idealism." But, whatever their motives may be, the Swiss consistently have been among the most humanitarian peoples in the world. Not only are Swiss citizens generously charitable, but the Government itself is liberal with donations. The International Committee of the Red Cross, which was a century old in 1963, is financed by voluntary contributions, a large proportion of them year after year furnished by the Swiss people. The Committee, which is the governing body of the International Red Cross, received its second Nobel Peace Prize on its 100th anniversary. Because its officials, being Swiss, have neutral diplomatic status, they are able to act internationally irrespective of political and military boundaries.

In time of war the Red Cross provides food, medical supplies and mail from home to soldiers in enemy prison camps, the distribution being supervised by its own personnel. During

World War II, a central tracing agency in Geneva amassed 35 million index cards for the identification of prisoners and missing civilians. Since 1945 the League of Red Cross Societies, which also has headquarters in Geneva, has distributed tons of food and medical supplies to people displaced and distressed by wars and revolutions in Palestine, Greece, Hungary, North Africa and the Congo, as well as to those left homeless by the Yugoslav earthquake of 1963. Other humanitarian enterprises have included gifts of cows to replenish Dutch herds after the disastrous floods of 1953 and a 1956 "freedom train" of Hungarians.

Switzerland's most disarming charity is the Pestalozzi Children's Village, named after the great 18th Century Swiss educator, Heinrich Pestalozzi. A cluster of 20 houses in the canton of Appenzell, the village is home for 250 orphans from 10 countries. Among the most recent to arrive were 22 young Tibetans from Indian refugee camps. They live in a new house that was built especially for them, and there they are educated according to Buddhist traditions. The smiling, doll-like children have won the hearts of the natives, and some of them have been taken into Swiss homes.

Possibly because Swiss adults have difficulty being open or affectionate with each other, they are remarkably tender with children. They also feel a deep compassion for animals. The swans on Swiss lakes are as carefully counted by census takers as are the Swiss people themselves. In the winter of 1962-1963, when the Lake of Zurich froze over for the first time in 35 years, radio reported that the birds were in distress. Within an hour the lake's shores were crowded with bird-lovers bearing bags of food.

THOUGH the democratic Swiss find any system of caste intolerable, they are, in fact, divided by wealth into a number of subtly gradated classes. While there is no proletariat in the usual European sense, and neither slums nor beggars are to be seen, the middle class equality of wealth which *seems* to extend over everyone is really a masquerade which all but a

few conspire to maintain. Switzerland does have a number of very wealthy men, and since wealth is the barometer of success in a mercantile world, a Swiss instinctively feels awe for those who earn more than he does and a kind of contempt for those less fortunate.

Mobility up the economic scale is slow in Switzerland. A farmer's son may become a schoolteacher and his son may become a professor, but the two steps could hardly be taken in one generation. In workers' districts one sometimes senses a resentment toward any one of the neighbors who rises above the group. Rather than be rejected by his family and his community, the individual may prefer to remain, or appear to remain, on the economic level into which he was born.

FOR men, the barriers of economic class break down completely during military service, when genuine friendships based on mutual interests are formed. As a school for citizenship and equality, the Army has a deep and lasting influence on every male Swiss. For many a Swiss, the annual three weeks of training is the happiest time of the year. It allows him to indulge his immoderate passion for shooting, not with Wilhelm Tell crossbows but with a *Sturmgewehr*, a highly efficient new submachine gun. It also provides a man with an opportunity to escape from the world of women, to flee the all-enveloping matriarchy which comes close to ruling him and his land.

After three weeks of military life, the Swiss soldier takes his *Sturmgewehr* and goes home. His quiet exaltation in the outdoor democratic male life is forgotten for another year, and the old class positions are resumed. Women hang their husbands' uniforms out to be aired, the wives of corporals and sergeants making sure that the uniforms' stripes are visibly displayed to the less fortunate wives whose husbands are merely privates. The men, riding the early trains to offices and factories, see the uniforms flapping on the lines and become aware of how completely they have been brought back to the oligarchy of women.

A Tradition of Urban Elegance

The sophisticated, urban side of Swiss life is sometimes overlooked in bursts of enthusiasm for the nation's economy, its scenery or its quaint customs. So many descriptions of Switzerland make it sound like clockwork—small, precise and mechanical. Such an analogy ignores the enlightened tradition in every city. Since the time of the 18th Century philosopher Jean Jacques Rousseau, Geneva has been the mother of—and hostess to—scores of thinkers and artists. Zurich has its artistic significance as well, although the outstanding aspect of this city is the driving pulse of its commercial life. Swiss cities are more than efficient and clean; they are also enthusiastic centers of culture.

LUNCHTIME BROWSERS examine books at a department store in the center of Zurich. A cultural capital of the country, Zurich is the headquarters for 60 book-publishing firms and for a dozen widely circulated daily and weekly newspapers.

CHILDREN'S CIRCUS in Zurich
plays to young audiences
and raises money for war orphans

DRUM MAJORETTES announce the start of Zurich's Kinder Cirkus Ullalla-Bassissi. The first two words in the name mean "children's circus"; the last two are magical nonsense.

SWAN BALLET fascinates an audience of children and their parents at the pavilion where the circus maintains its headquarters. The troupe also goes on tour through the nation.

COSTUMED RINGMASTER, a girl disguised in a top hat describes the act to follow. The amateur circus has grown from a troupe of 30 to one of 300 children since its birth in 1953.

GRAND FINALE arrives *(below)* as a performer balances on a ladder. Proceeds from the shows go to the Pestalozzi Children's Village, a welfare center for war orphans in Appenzell canton.

NEIGHBORLY GREETINGS are offered by ambling shoppers who come to the farmers' market held in Yverdon twice a week. Fruits and flowers deck the stalls and fill the wicker baskets in this small city in the heart of the nation's farmland.

SYSTEMATIC SEARCH for a designated item *(left)* is aided by the organized arrangement of counters at Zurich's Jelmoli, largest department store in Switzerland. Above the counter is a hand-decorated scarf which hangs on a metal display rack.

GARDEN APPLIANCES fill a window of the Thun branch of the Migros chain *(opposite)*. A cut-rate empire of vast supermarkets, the chain was founded by the late Gottlieb Duttweiler and is now owned cooperatively by patrons and employees.

SHOPPING *at rural markets and metropolitan shops is geared to suit any taste*

BILINGUAL PERIODICALS, in both German and French, attract an audience to a kiosk in Zurich's major park, the Zurichhorn. A high proportion of Swiss speak more than one language, and one out of every 10 persons in the country is a foreigner.

SUN WORSHIPERS while away a summer afternoon lounging beneath a modern statue on the grass at the Zurichhorn. Nearby is the Tiefenbrunnen Lido, an elaborate beach development. The Zurichhorn is less than a mile from downtown Zurich.

LEISURE TIME in the city provides young pleasure seekers with a chance for agreeable diversions

SYMPATHETIC SPECTATORS watch men fishing from the banks of the Rhine in Basel, a flourishing metropolis whose strategic river location makes it one of the most prosperous in Europe. The sign on the wharf advertises river excursions.

SALOON STEAMER, a Lake of Lucerne pleasure boat at the water's edge looms up behind a little boy who is feeding the swans. Boating, the mountain scenery and excellent lake-front hotels make Lucerne the most frequented of all Swiss resorts.

6

A High Sensibility

"THE Italian Renaissance," said Orson Welles in the film *The Third Man*, "was full of crimes and excesses, and yet it gave us the greatest masterpieces of art . . . Switzerland has lived in peace for three centuries and what has she given us? The cuckoo clock."

Aside from being wrong in fact—cuckoo clocks are made in Germany's Schwarzwald district—this famous denunciation of Switzerland is wrong also in its implication. One of the most unjust although widely accepted canards of our time is that the Swiss are uncultured.

The Swiss are, as a matter of fact, among the most enthusiastically cultured people in the world. Unfortunately, because of the unique character of Swiss culture, it has never been properly understood, not even by the Swiss themselves, who, suffering from a national inferiority complex, are apt to accept without protest the world's judgment.

The Swiss lack of cultural snobbery is perhaps inevitable in a small country which has always been a democracy, which has never had a royal court or an imperial capital to centralize creativity, where there were few splendid noblemen to disperse fortunes in the patronage of artists. In the absence of noble patrons, the role of fostering creativity has fallen upon the citizenry. Swiss culture is preeminently the culture of a democracy. Lacking an elite to foster a highbrow, aristocratic culture, it has also lacked the proletarian taste which develops what has come in recent years to be called popular culture. Swiss culture does not boast a series of creative peaks like the cultures of other nations; it is a plateau of consistently high averages. It is characterized especially by a wide popular interest in every sort of cultural enterprise rather than by outbursts of volcanic genius. More, perhaps, than the average man in any other European country, the Swiss is familiar with the achievements of his own artists and aware of the world's cultural climate. The Swiss respect for learning is also unusual. For centuries bourgeois Swiss families have taken pride in encouraging at least one son to turn his back on worldly gain and pursue an academic career while his brothers manage the family business.

THIS urge to nourish, protect and appreciate the arts extends down to the native music and dance, costumes and handicrafts of the Swiss countryside. And Switzerland is particularly rich in folk arts. The nostalgic lyrics that accompany yodeling songs in north and central Switzerland and the folk songs of Vaud retain their traditional purity. The sprightly folk dances and the colorful dancers' costumes that express the gayer side of the Swiss character have been passed down from generation to generation. The country people cling to their painted cupboards, chests and hand-carved cradles. They also zealously preserve the country's indigenous styles of architecture. The brown-beamed farmhouses of eastern Switzerland with their mottoes and crests, the balconied chalets of Schwyz and the frescoed stucco houses of the Grisons and the Rhine villages have changed little in five centuries.

At the other end of the cultural scale the Swiss have preserved a long tradition of humanistic learning. The monastery of St. Gall, founded in memory of an Irish monk, was one of the great centers of learning during the reign of Charlemagne. There in the Ninth Century a monk named Notker Le Bègue wrote his magnificent Gregorian chants. In the 16th Century Basel became a center of the Renaissance. Two great painters worked there, Hans Holbein and the Swiss Urs Graf, and the humanist Erasmus lived and wrote there between 1521 and 1529. Separated only by the Rhine from Germany, Basel has remained a Swiss center of Germanic culture to the present day. The Swiss-born historian of the Renaissance, Jakob Burckhardt, and the German philosopher, Friedrich Nietzsche, were 19th Century colleagues in Basel University, where in the present century Karl Barth was professor of theology.

A SECOND liberal "French" school of Swiss intellectualism and art developed in Geneva about 1800. Spurred by the writings of Jean Jacques Rousseau, the Geneva group developed around the cosmopolitan personalities of Madame Germaine de Staël, the daughter of a powerful Swiss banker, and her passionate lover, Benjamin Constant, both of whom wrote romantic novels. The French philosopher and wit Voltaire, who lived in exile near Geneva for many years, had this to say of his adopted town: "There is no other city which has more spirited citizens or more philosophers."

Swiss intellectual and esthetic life is nourished by two roots: nature and the political community. Despite their industrialization, the Swiss have never broken with nature and the soil. Such loyalty to roots has influenced all their arts and letters. In the 15th Century, painter Konrad Witz made the Lake of Geneva the setting for his *Miraculous Draught of Fishes,* and ever since Swiss artists have been predominantly nature painters. In the 19th Century, Albert Anker painted realistic scenes of peasant life, and his even greater contemporary, Ferdinand Hodler, painted his allegories and haunting, monumental figures against backgrounds of stark mountains and glaciers.

Literature has been equally bound to nature. In the 18th Century a group of writers, Rousseau among them, wrote lyrically of the Alps and their inhabitants. A famous pair of 19th Century novelists, Jeremias Gotthelf and Gottfried Keller, wrote rustic novels of village people. Johanna Spyri's beloved *Heidi* takes place largely, of course, in the Alps.

Switzerland's most eminent novelist of the 20th Century, the late Charles Ferdinand Ramuz, said of Swiss writers: "Poets they may be, but first and foremost they are voters." As with every Swiss—mountain herdsman, railroad conductor or bank president—the Swiss artist and writer is spurred in his life's work by a sense of service to his country. Indeed, many have combined public service with their artistic pursuits. Niklaus Manuel, a writer-painter of the Reformation, was a *Landvogt,* or magistrate, in Bern. An 18th Century nature poet, Albrecht von Haller, was a physician, botanist and Bern bureaucrat; the novelist Gotthelf was a Zwinglian minister and his contemporary Gottfried Keller served with distinction as secretary of the canton of Zurich. It was Keller who said: "Woe to him who does not bind his fate to that of the public community, for not only will he find no rest, but he will lose all inner strength and will be abandoned to the disdain of the people, like a weed growing by the way."

THIS awareness that creativity is rooted in nature and history is both an inspiration for and an inhibitor of Swiss art and literature. Love of country, it is true, can spur an artist to great achievements, but the world's greatest masterpieces have been the work of men with a still higher loyalty to the eternal truths of the human heart or to God. In addition, the bourgeois Swiss, with their passion for equality, have little use for the lavishness and ostentation which has sometimes inspired and often accompanied the world's great art. They tend to be suspicious of anything which surpasses the average, and rather than single out an exceptional individual, they desire to raise the average. It has been said that in Switzerland talent is admissible but genius is intolerable.

If this intangible but nonetheless real atmosphere turns the Swiss toward conservation and study of the old rather than the creation of the new, there are also more tangible forces which do the same thing. As with business and government, the direction of art in Switzerland is not toward concentration but dispersal. Politically Switzerland has turned its complexity of minorities into a strength. But in a country so diversified in languages, religions and traditions, any sort of cultural homogeneity is impossible. For the artist and intellectual the lack of a common rallying point poses problems of identity which many have solved by alliances with other countries.

SURROUNDED as they are by three of the most dynamic cultures in Europe, Swiss artists and writers cannot help but respond to the forces these other cultures exert. From this situation, in part, comes the myth that Switzerland has produced few if any creative men: The country's most renowned cultural figures have so often sought inspiration in, and have ultimately become so identified with, the cultural traditions of other countries that people often forget that they were originally Swiss. The great Renaissance painter Hans Holbein, for example, made his home in Basel where he executed many fine religious paintings, but he is best known for the portraits of Henry VIII and his entourage which he did after he had been named official painter to the English court. Three centuries later Arnold Böcklin, a Swiss painter famous for his classical allegories set in natural surroundings, was inspired by the cultural heritage of Italy, where he spent much of his life.

Even today the trend continues. Although he was born in Neuchâtel, Le Corbusier is commonly thought of as France's leading architect, and more of his imaginative and graceful structures have been built in France and even India than in Switzerland. One of the most highly regarded of living sculptors, Alberto Giacometti, whose elongated bronze human figures can be seen in most of the world's museums of modern art, was also born in Switzerland, although he lives in, and is identified with,

Paris. The late Paul Klee, Switzerland's greatest modern painter, is commonly associated with 20th Century German schools of art.

Painters, sculptors and architects who work with material things are freer for such cultural roamings than writers who are imprisoned by language. Nevertheless, France and Germany have virtually absorbed many of Switzerland's great writers, beginning with Rousseau, who lived most of his life in France and is buried in the Pantheon in Paris. He is invariably grouped with the French philosophers of the 18th Century. Novelist Gottfried Keller, a poetic realist, is considered one of the greatest German-language writers of the 19th Century, as is Conrad Ferdinand Meyer, who turned to the histories of England, France and Italy for his subject matter. The historian Jakob Burckhardt, widely known for *The Culture of the Renaissance,* which was inspired by years of residence in Italy, had a conflicting loyalty to Germany and once said: "I would like to devote my life to teaching the Swiss that they are Germans."

The two foremost German-language playwrights living today, Friedrich Dürrenmatt and Max Frisch, are both Swiss. Although the former has remained in his native country, his writing derives from the German tradition of grotesque fantasy, showing the influence of Franz Kafka and Bertolt Brecht. He has rejected the ordered external world of his countrymen to deal with the violent world of crime and guilt which he feels lies behind it. His most famous play, *The Visit,* exposes the rapaciousness and ruthlessness of human nature when men are tempted by wealth. Frisch ridicules the secure but narrow-minded citizens of small countries like his own, and yearns for a wider, more spacious, more significant world.

P ARTLY because so many Swiss writers have used either French or German, a great many people believe that Switzerland has no national language. While there are four official languages —German, French, Italian and Romansch—the national language, spoken by 70 per cent of the people, is Schwyzerdütsch. Though there are many regional dialects of this Swiss-German, it is itself not a dialect but a branch of Alemannic, a language spoken in Switzerland and southern Germany for more than a thousand years. To outsiders the guttural mumblings of this Swiss language may sound like an epiglottic disease. For those who understand it, Schwyzerdütsch is uncommonly pithy and forceful —a fountain of picturesque speech. Zwingli's Bible, published in 1525, is in the Swiss language, and for the past century several generations of lexicographers have been compiling *Das Schweizerische Idiotikon,* a Swiss dictionary of which part has already been published. Swiss words used by the two most famous German-language novelists, Gotthelf and Keller, have become part of the language of written German. The Swiss feel that their language is one of their strongest shields against foreign penetration, an efficient weapon in the preservation of their cultural and political independence.

W ITH their sense of social and political responsibility, Swiss cultural leaders tend to consider themselves primarily educators. Burckhardt, Karl Barth and Carl Jung have all been professors. It is not surprising, then, that one of the leading formulators of modern educational methods was a Swiss, Johann Heinrich Pestalozzi, whose influence on elementary teaching is still alive today.

Pestalozzi's premise was that a child's education should consist of opportunities to develop its natural gifts in an atmosphere free from the corrupting influences of civilization. To put his theories into practice Pestalozzi took a group of orphan children to a farm near Zurich, which he turned into the world's first progressive school. The experiment went bankrupt, but some years later Pestalozzi founded another orphanage in the canton of Unterwalden. When this was closed by authorities to be turned into a military hospital, Pestalozzi started again in the neighborhood of Bern.

In his last enterprise, in a castle in the canton of Vaud, Pestalozzi devoted himself primarily to the training of teachers. All this time he was writing vigorously, spreading his theories that civilization could be saved by education and that only unselfish love could produce unselfish beings. The function of education was to develop not intellectuals but citizens, and this was to be accomplished by cultivating the free and natural personalities of children.

By the time of Pestalozzi's death in 1827, his fame as "the elementary schoolteacher of mankind" had spread throughout Europe and England. The Swiss, their interest in education spurred, have set up one of the finest educational systems in the world, rivaling the celebrated French and German systems on which it is largely based.

The high quality of Swiss education extends to seven universities and a number of specialized institutions including the influential Jung Institute of psychiatry in Zurich, and Zurich's Federal Institute of Technology, famous for its colony of Nobel Prize winners.

A people so well educated are equipped to continue through life their pursuit of knowledge. To keep informed, every Swiss reads a great deal with interest and with profit. An American who encountered a Swiss architect recently was astounded by the breadth of the young man's interests. He not only followed avidly the work of architects all over the world, but the work of writers, painters and philosophers as well. He was so intimately acquainted with the latest projects of Swiss authors that it seemed he must have been eavesdropping at every literary café in Switzerland simultaneously.

TO feed such extraordinary cultural hunger, Swiss publishers issue more than 4,500 new titles each year. Most publishers are located in Zurich, which is a publishing center for Germany and Austria as well. With more than 1,600 periodicals, Switzerland is the most newspaper-surfeited country in the world. Zurich's venerated *Neue Zürcher Zeitung* is perhaps the most famous of all German-language newspapers; its impartial and liberal coverage of the news during this century's two world wars won for it a large international following.

The leading weekly journal, *Die Weltwoche*, and the elegantly printed monthly journal of culture, called *Du*, have world-wide circulations. Even small-town papers give wide coverage to international news. Their old-fashioned appearance is misleading, for they are mature, honest and courageously outspoken. The ethical standards of Swiss broadcasting are high—Government-controlled television broadcasts chamber concerts and operas as well as plays by Strindberg and Brecht.

SWITZERLAND is bursting with art treasures that are rarely known to the businessman who comes to make deals or the tourist who pursues snowy peaks and chalet-dotted Alpine meadows. The Swiss, however, are well aware of them. On Sundays and holidays they jam the museums of Basel, which are treasuries of early German painting and Holbeins. They also flood the galleries of Bern, Geneva, Zurich, Schaffhausen and a dozen other cities. The Swiss are compulsive collectors—it is safe to say that they own more art per person than any other people. Among the great private art collections open to the public are the Bührle collection of Zurich, the Sacher collection in Basel, the Reinhart collection in Winterthur, the Hahnloser and Rupf collections in Bern and the Müller collection in Solothurn. The owners of these collections have a reverential feeling about their paintings and sometimes resent visitors rushing through their galleries without showing proper appreciation.

A natural development in an art-conscious industrial land is the advertising poster. Such great painters as Cuno Amiet, Ferdinand Hodler and the contemporary Hans Erni have devoted much of their best work to the "art of the streets." In the processes of color printing the Swiss have no match. Such firms as Skira print faultless reproductions and by far the most beautiful art books in the world.

The art in which the Swiss are especially appreciative and knowledgeable is music. Geneva's conductor, Ernest Ansermet, is famous for his interpretations of the work of modern composers. Zurich has 10 concert halls, 53 male choruses and 560 music professors. The city's attitude toward music is indicated in an apocryphal story of a visiting gentleman who accosted a beautiful streetwalker near the concert hall and was told "Not tonight. They're performing the *Missa Solemnis* of Beethoven." Zurich's state-sponsored opera house is famous for producing modern and experimental works by Hindemith, Honegger, Bloch, Stravinsky, Berg, Schoenberg and Kodaly. Honegger and Bloch, two of the 20th Century's most remarkable composers, are both of Swiss origin, although like so many other Swiss artists they are identified with other countries (Honegger with France and Bloch with the United States).

Opera singers come to Switzerland from more than a dozen nations. Among the world-famous artists whose careers were fostered in Zurich are the husband-and-wife team from America, James McCracken and Sandra Warfield. On one recent evening McCracken was singing *Otello* in the opera house while his contralto wife was performing a Brahms song cycle in the Tonhalle across the Limmat, and both halls were sold out. The McCrackens have bought a house outside Zurich and have taken up permanent residence there. Of the Swiss people McCracken says, "I have never sung before warmer audiences. In no country in the world is a singer so respected and loved. Our status is something like Mickey Mantle's and Elizabeth Taylor's in America."

THE Swiss compulsion to turn knowledge into reality, and the guilty feeling that leisure and spiritual vagabondage are an unpatriotic waste of time, may be handicaps to a poet. They are not for the scientist who is contentedly aware that he is serving the human community. As a result, when a Swiss has a great vision he is less likely to write a poem or a novel than he is to design a great bridge, like New York's George Washington, built by the Swiss engineer Othman Ammann. In the roster of Nobel Prizes, the Swiss can claim 14 winners, nine of them in the fields of science and medicine.

Switzerland's great scientists include an 18th Century group of Basel mathematicians, the Bernoulli family and Leonhard Euler; the Bernese poet-anatomist Albrecht von Haller; and the 19th Century naturalist Louis Agassiz. Agassiz emigrated to the United States and was instrumental in making Harvard conscious that a great modern university should be a center of scientific as well as humanistic studies. In the 20th Century Switzerland gave asylum and citizenship to Albert Einstein and produced another top-rank nuclear physicist in Zurich-born Felix Bloch. The most famous pioneering explorers of both the heights and the depths are the brothers Auguste and Jean Piccard, who were born in Basel.

PARTLY because of this same inbred preference for concrete conceptions, Swiss thinkers tend to be theologians whose work has immediate relevance to the lives of the people, rather than philosophers. Among the most influential 20th Century Christian thinkers are the Swiss Protestants Karl Barth and Emil Brunner and the Roman Catholic Hans Küng, who was one of the most influential voices during the second Vatican Council. The great psychoanalyst Carl Jung's work and thought developed toward the end of his long life into something much like a religious quest.

Only two Swiss Nobel Prize winners have been men of literature—poet Carl Spitteler in 1919 and the Swiss-naturalized novelist Hermann Hesse in 1946. However, in the last two decades Switzerland has rocketed to an unprecedented literary eminence in the field of drama with Friedrich Dürrenmatt and Max Frisch. In a ringing statement of his faith in all mankind, Frisch has evoked the spirit of all Swiss scientists, thinkers and artists:

"Our home is man; to him above all belongs our allegiance; in the fact that fatherland and mankind do not mutually exclude themselves, in that actually consists the happiness of being the son of a small country."

Dr. Carl Jung, one of the most influential pioneers in analytical psychology, works in his study at Küsnacht. Jung died at 85 in 1961.

Bold Searchers for New Paths in Thought and Art

If the Swiss people can be accused of being conservative and complacent, their artists and thinkers have been, and are, boldly original. The psychologist Carl Jung was a leader in the movement which revolutionized man's concept of his own nature. Modern Swiss theologians are critically reappraising the role of Christianity in the modern world. In the arts, two dramatists, Max Frisch and Friedrich Dürrenmatt, have joined the painter Paul Klee in fashioning new, decisive images through which men everywhere can better understand themselves.

ROMAN CATHOLIC LIBERAL, Hans Küng chats after lecturing to a class at the University of Tübingen in West Germany. Küng has been a leader of the Church's reform movement.

PROTESTANT THEOLOGIAN, Karl Barth meets with students from the University of Basel. Barth's massive *Church Dogmatics* emphasizes the role of faith in winning salvation.

PASSIONATE SATIRIST, Max Frisch *(opposite)* draws wryly on his pipe. Both a novelist and dramatist, he is best known in the U.S. for his drama *The Firebugs,* a political allegory.

MORDANT HUMORIST, Friedrich Dürrenmatt, the famous Swiss playwright, discusses his work in his Neuchâtel home. His play *The Visit* was a great success in Europe and America.

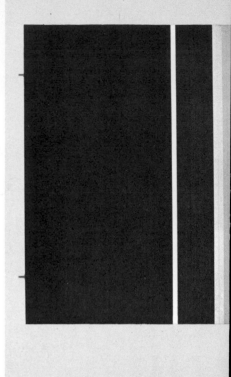

VERSATILE PAINTER who has done distinguished work in a wide variety of fields, Hans Erni works on a design spread on his studio floor. Erni's paintings are frequently exhibited and he has done murals, illustrated books and designed posters.

GRAPHICS flourish
as gifted men bring
the standards of fine art
to commercial design

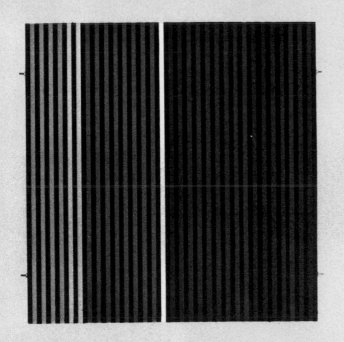

BRILLIANT NEWCOMER, young Karl Gerstner, seen with three of his works, is a successful advertising artist whose posters are represented in several museums of art. Good applied design has been fostered by Swiss art schools for five decades.

PRIZE-WINNING DESIGNER, Josef Müller-Brockmann works with models as he ponders a problem involving three dimensions. He has turned his hand to stage sets, advertising and book design and has lectured in both the U.S. and Japan.

97

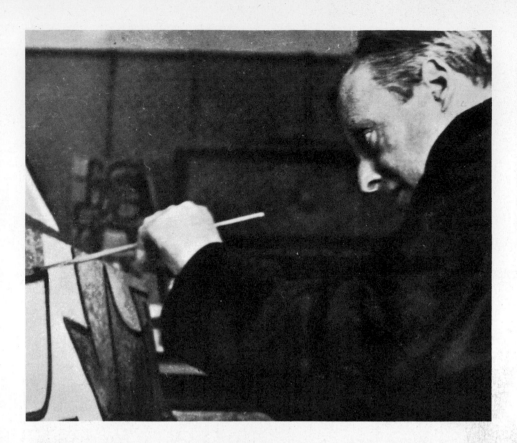

PAUL KLEE is known for his precise, wryly humorous paintings

INVENTIVE CRAFTSMAN, Klee carefully works on a canvas in his Bern studio in 1939 *(left)*. Klee used both oil and watercolors and was a master of the graphic arts.

WITTY PAINTING called *Nearly Hit (opposite)* evokes in a few swift, expressive lines the shock and surprise of a pedestrian who has barely escaped being run down.

RELAXED ARTIST, turns his intense but humorous gaze on his wife, Lily, as they sit in their garden with Klee's father *(below)*. Both Klee and his father died in 1940.

7

The Mountain Playground

THE visitor to Switzerland who expects to be greeted at the village railroad station by the yodelers and winsome girls in lacy hats he has seen on travel posters is in for a disappointment. "In our modern industrial country," said the playwright Friedrich Dürrenmatt, "the simpering milkmaid and the alphorn are about as valid national images as the gangster and gun-toting cowboy are in America. In our case, the hoax is perpetrated by our tourist officials."

On the other hand, the mountains on the posters are very real indeed. There is hardly a spot in southern Switzerland where the visitor does not find himself overawed by one or two

or half a dozen magnificent snow-topped peaks. Switzerland's tourist business began when the Swiss discovered there was foreign gold to be mined in those hills. Other countries have tried to turn scenery into an "export," but none has succeeded quite so adroitly as Switzerland.

As late as the 18th Century, travelers in Switzerland were still clinging to the gentle shores of the lakes of Neuchâtel and Biel. The crags, peaks and gorges of the Alps were considered grotesqueries of nature. Swiss peasants, struggling to wrest a living from the rugged and sterile landscape, looked upon the mountains as enemies and believed them infested with a whole spook mythology of dragons, witches and abominable snowmen who caused avalanches, lightning and flash floods. In the 16th Century there had been some ascents, including Leonardo da Vinci's climb of Monte Viso, to study minerals and plant life, but the explorations had little effect on the public.

The notion that mountains are monstrous excrescences in nature began to fade when a number of 18th Century scientists who were searching for fossils and plant and insect specimens began to be aware of the mountains as personalities. In 1729 the Bern naturalist Albrecht von Haller published a poem called "The Alps" praising the mountains' magnificence. By creating a new genre of poetry, the nature poem, Haller opened the eyes of his countrymen to the beauties of the Swiss landscape.

A quarter of a century later his case was taken up by Jean Jacques Rousseau. The philosopher, whose *Nouvelle Héloïse* and *Emile* had made the shores of the Lake of Geneva a mecca for esthetic pilgrims, now urged a return to the natural surroundings of Innerschweiz, to the frugal pastoral life of the Alps.

The next and most crucial chapter in the history of Alpinism was written by the Genevese physicist Horace Benedict de Saussure. De Saussure began geological explorations into the highlands in 1760. After crossing the Alps on foot he felt an urge to climb Mont Blanc on the Italian-French border. For 27 years the mountain frustrated his efforts. But his failures only increased de Saussure's obsession. When he finally triumphed in 1787, he wrote, "The instant in which I reached the highest point of the snow that crowns the peak, I stamped on it in rage rather than with a pleasurable

ADVENTURERS on a natural history expedition are shown in a 19th Century etching as they cling to the face of a cliff in the Alps and collect early geographical data.

sensation. . . . It seemed to be that I alone had survived the universe and that I was seeing its corpse spread out beneath my feet."

With these words de Saussure articulated for the first time the ambivalent mixture of love and hate which climbers have felt for mountains ever since. While Haller had "discovered" the Alps and Rousseau had stirred a new enthusiasm for nature, de Saussure invented Alpinism and became the patron of mountaineers.

His experience seemed to unleash a hidden yearning for heights in the Anglo-Saxon heart, for it was British climbers who rallied to Switzerland and inaugurated mountaineering's golden age. By the late 19th Century, Englishmen had climbed almost every Alpine summit. The most famous ascent was made on July 14, 1865, up the forbidding 14,698-foot Matterhorn by a 26-year-old London artist named Edward Whymper who had failed in seven previous attempts. On this eighth try he was accompanied by three other Britons and three Swiss guides. They set out on July 13, camped overnight halfway up, and reached the summit the next day at 1:40 p.m. After an hour of admiring the view, the seven men roped themselves together for the descent. Minutes later one of the Englishmen slipped, the rope broke and all the men but Whymper and two of the guides were hurled 4,000 feet to their deaths.

The publicity given this tragedy surprisingly heated rather than chilled the public's imagination, and the Matterhorn became the Olympus of mountaineers. More than 100,000 persons have climbed it since Whymper's ascent and nearly 100 have lost their lives. In Zermatt, the village at the foot of the mountain, a small Anglican cemetery is almost entirely given over to the remains of English victims of the Matterhorn. By the time the pioneer English climbers moved on to the higher peaks of South America and Asia, the Swiss themselves had become ardent Alpinists. It has been estimated that there are 25,000 active climbers in Switzerland and the leading mountaineering club, the Club Alpin Suisse, numbers 45,000 members.

With their new interest in mountaineering, the Swiss developed a passion for "belvederes." A belvedere is an Alpine ledge which is reached by a cog railway or aerial cable car and which has an awesome view and a hotel. Best known is the Rigi, which overlooks the Lake of Lucerne. The classic 19th Century Grand Tour always included an overnight stay on the Rigi to witness a sunrise. Mark Twain, aroused for the spectacle at 3 a.m., missed it by making the mistake of facing west instead of east. But a Victorian lady named Miss Jemima Morell, a member of the first European tour organized by Thomas Cook in 1863, compared the vision to "the New Jerusalem as seen by the exiled John from the great high mountain, descending out of heaven from God, prepared as a bride adorned for her husband."

EXCURSIONISTS travel across the Lake of Lucerne in a paddle-wheel steamer around 1890. Viewing the surrounding mountains from the water was as popular then as now.

Having firmly established climbing as a sport, the English next introduced skiing. A Norwegian had demonstrated the use of skis in Winterthur in 1889, but it remained for the British to popularize the sport. In 1894 Sir Arthur Conan Doyle, creator of Sherlock Holmes, published his account of a Swiss ski journey, and after that, Englishmen introduced skiing at Grindelwald in the canton of Bern and at Davos and St. Moritz in the Grisons. Bobsledding and tobogganing were already well established, however, and they remained popular winter sports until after World War I, when a growing interest in skiing brought it into first place.

Today, it has been estimated, half the adults in Switzerland are skiers. The Alps have been mechanized with 382 ski lifts and at several of the larger resorts, including Gstaad, Mürren, St. Moritz and Zermatt, crack skiers go in for glacier skiing, for which they are flown to the tops of the glaciers in small airplanes.

While they were learning from the English how to turn their scenery into revenue, the Swiss were transforming another natural resource, their water power, into transportation. During the 19th Century they started to build one of the world's most advanced railroad networks which, lacking coal, they early began to electrify. By 1961 all of Switzerland's 3,450 miles of track were electrified. Today the country's transportation system includes 875 electric locomotives, 672 tunnels and 5,129 bridges. In addition to the railroads, there is a fleet of 113 steamers which carry more than 11 million passengers a year on the Swiss lakes.

The Swiss have fallen behind only in highway construction. In the 1930s they had a more than adequate system of roads, but with the enormous postwar increase in native and foreign automobiles, their highways have become woefully inadequate. What to do about the situation is one of the major political headaches for cantonal and Confederation legislators. Nevertheless, some progress is being made. The first automobile tunnel through the Alps, the recently opened Grand St. Bernard, has cut an afternoon's driving time from the trip between Switzerland's northern cities and Italy, and a new national motor network, begun in 1960, is scheduled to be finished by 1970.

In the air, however, the Swiss have not lagged behind. Swissair, the national airline, which began with 13 primitive aircraft in 1931, today has a fleet of 18 massive jetliners and 15 propeller-driven passenger planes which bind the landlocked Swiss with 41 foreign countries. The famous high standard of Swissair comfort and service is the result of a conscious effort to duplicate the atmosphere of a Swiss hotel.

IN the science and art of hotel management the Swiss have no peers. The heyday of splendid *Arabian Nights* palaces such as the Suvretta in St. Moritz, when Russian dukes and Indian maharajas arrived with entourages of servants and sycophants, is gone forever. A few of the elegant luxury hotels, however, survive. A half dozen are recognized as the true aristocrats among the world's hotels: the Palace in St. Moritz, now with a regular clientele of international socialites rather than royalty; Bürgenstock's Palace on a belvedere over the Lake of Lucerne; the Three Kings in Basel, Switzerland's leading businessman's hotel; the Bellevue Palace in Bern, with a superb view of the Alps and a clientele made up largely of diplomats; the Schweizerhof in Lucerne, which maintains its well-known Victorian elegance; and the Beau-Rivage in the Ouchy district of Lausanne, long a favorite of exiled nobility.

Life is luxurious and unhurried for both guests and managers in such pleasure domes as these. The life of the average Swiss hotelier, who struggles to accommodate busloads of querulous tourists organized for one-night stays by travel agencies, is not as sweet. Another headache is the labor shortage. Hotel workers are being recruited in Germany, Italy, Spain, Greece and even Algeria. The resulting linguistic confusion is exasperating for both hoteliers and their guests. Still, most of the hotels manage to maintain a warm and friendly atmosphere. Usually small, with fewer than 100 beds, the Swiss hotel is more like a gracious and civilized home than like the huge and impersonal hostelries characteristic of U.S. cities.

Swiss hotels are almost invariably notable for both service and cuisine. Much of the credit for their excellence must go to the country's hotel schools. The oldest and most famous is the *Ecole Hôtelière de la Société Suisse des Hôteliers* in Lausanne. There, 300 young men and women from 25 countries are taught to keep books, plan menus, calculate food costs, chill and decant wine, make beds, arrange flowers, and welcome guests in at least three languages. Some of Switzerland's vocational high schools put fledgling cooks through rigorous three-year courses during which they learn to prepare the country's most famous specialties.

The tourist industry, employing 140,000 people, stands second after machine tools among Swiss "exports." Any fluctuation is felt at once by the sensitively geared Swiss economy. In the country's delicate balance of trade, the $300 million contributed by tourism in a peak year has covered 33 per cent of the gap between Switzerland's exports and imports. The French historian André Siegfried speaks of tourists depositing their riches in "the same way as the traditional inundations of the Nile fertilize the Delta." The largesse not only is spread over hotels and restaurants, railways and airlines, but indirectly helps finance schools and hospitals. It is a rare visitor to Switzerland who does not buy a watch or a camera, and two ancient Swiss crafts—the lacemaking and embroidery of St. Gall and the woodcarving of Brienz—are now patronized almost exclusively by tourists.

IF tourists now flock to Switzerland for the scenery, the fine hotels, the skiing or the chance to scale a peak, it was not so long ago that a sadder and quieter type of visitor made up a significant part of the country's guest list. These were the sick—most of them people with tuberculosis who came to heal their infected lungs in the pure and rarefied mountain air. Now that antibiotics can almost invariably cure this once dreaded and often fatal disease, few victims of TB come to Switzerland, but there was a time when the country's most barren canton, the Grisons, was a busy and profitable international health resort with sanitariums, many of them very elaborate, perched on virtually every Alpine hillside. An unforgettable picture of life in these retreats is given in Thomas Mann's great novel *The Magic Mountain*.

A few of the sanitariums now care for people suffering from asthma; others have been turned into ski resorts where—such is the beneficence of modern medicine—apple cheeks indicate a fast run on a windy ski slope rather than the macabre false-health that often attended the last stages of tuberculosis.

Switzerland has traditionally provided a haven not only for the sick but also for those escaping political disorders. The neutral, liberty-loving Swiss have for centuries given refuge to exiles fleeing revolutions and persecution in other lands. One of the first was Voltaire, whose incessant gibes at his French contemporaries had made residence in France distinctly dangerous for him. While he lived near Geneva, Voltaire amused himself by puckishly urging the puritanical elders of the city, who believed that anything which had to do with the stage was a work of Satan, to open a municipal theater. Another occasionally fractious literary guest was James Joyce, who fled Austria for neutral Zurich when World War I began. On one occasion Joyce, with Irish temper and tenacity, availed himself of the full machinery of Swiss law to fight out a case involving the cost of a pair of trousers.

Switzerland has, in fact, been the temporary home of a staggering number of writers, most of them escaping one sort of persecution or another at home. Byron, the German poet Rainer Maria Rilke, Thomas Mann, the poet-playwright Bertolt Brecht and a dozen others have lived there, including the amazingly prolific Belgian detective-story writer Georges Simenon. Mary Shelley unaccountably wrote *Frankenstein* while living in tranquil Geneva.

Musicians, too, have sought refuge, or simply peace and quiet, in Switzerland, the most notable among them being Johannes Brahms, Richard Wagner, Franz Lehar, Bruno Walter, Igor Stravinsky and Paul Hindemith. And the country continues to be a refuge for royal exiles. Former Kings Michael of Romania and Farouk of Egypt have lived there, as have members of the former ruling families of Italy and Spain. Reminding one not of the courtly past but of the difficult present are the ghosts of two other famous refugees to Switzerland, Vladimir Ilich Lenin and Leon Trotsky, whose spirits, angry and intense, perhaps still walk the streets of Geneva arguing about the best way to bring about the fall of the Czar.

Many of the glamorous or notorious refugees of today, however, are from the world of entertainment. A list of those who have residences in Switzerland might include Charlie Chaplin, Yul Brynner, Peter Ustinov, Orson Welles, William Holden and Noel Coward, all of whom live in or near Lausanne; Richard Burton, who has a house in Geneva, and Elizabeth Taylor, who has one in Gstaad; Mel Ferrer and Audrey Hepburn, who occupy a chalet on the Bürgenstock; and Deborah Kerr and Anatole Litvak, who have residences in Klosters.

One of Switzerland's attractions for such highly paid artists was the fact that becoming official residents of the country allowed them to escape the worst rigors of the United States's or British income taxes. To show the advantages of Swiss residence, at least until a change was made in the U.S. tax law in 1962, a tax lawyer once created a fictional actress who, for the purposes of this book, we will call Marion

---

THE FINE SKI SLOPES OF THE ALPS

The Swiss Alps offer the skier more advantages than any other ski center in the world. Other ski areas have some of Switzerland's advantages, but none can boast all of them. First, the majority of Alpine slopes are above the timber line and thus wide open. Second, slopes abound to suit every skier, from expert to novice; Davos alone has 48 runs. There are 125 resorts to choose from, and more than 100 ski schools. Snow conditions are excellent most winters and on high slopes, skiing lasts into June. Many ski runs end at the doorsteps of the resort hotels—and the hotels are hospitable and well-run, with lively *après-ski* activities and good food. Ski lifts are inexpensive and ever-present. Even the snowstorms seem to cooperate for the visitor's pleasure, for snow tends to fall at night, leaving the days brilliant, sunny and brisk.

Morgan. Marion, said the lawyer, even though she lived and earned her money in another country, not only could establish residence in Switzerland but also could incorporate herself as the Morgan Corporation in some Swiss canton. When Hollywood paid Marion a million dollars to star in films, the money was transferred to the Morgan Corporation, which paid a corporate tax to the canton; this seldom exceeded two tenths of 1 per cent, or $2,000. From the corporation Marion drew her running expenses, say $5,000 a month, on which she paid a normal Swiss tax. If Marion had filed a U.S. tax return on the million dollars, she would have had to pay up to $870,000, depending on her deductions and write-offs. In Switzerland her taxes on the million dollars would perhaps be less than 10 per cent of this.

THE Swiss take great pride in the presence of these wealthy and famous people in their land. They feel less warm toward the affluent postwar West Germans who have succeeded in what Hitler's armies never achieved—the occupation of Switzerland's "sun porch," the canton of Ticino.

Traditionally a poor canton with little industry, the Ticino was invaded about 1950 by a surge of Teutonic tourists. Advertisements in German newspapers offered land "far away from strategic targets, in a country which offers security, peace and order." More than 20 German real-estate firms began speculation in Ticinese properties, with the result that prices skyrocketed as much as 500 per cent. On the highways German automobiles became almost as numerous as Swiss, and Ticinese shopkeepers took crash courses in the German language. In an editorial, the Hamburg weekly *Die Zeit* pointed out that it was less sunshine and immunity from atom bombs that was luring Germans south than it was tax evasion and a "*Dolce Vita* on Lago Maggiore."

Not surprisingly, since an influx of money was involved, the Swiss were rather slow to react. In 1961 the National Assembly in Bern passed a law subjecting all land negotiations with foreigners to Government approval. The law has not greatly hindered the invasion. In a recent year 682 foreigners bought land in the Ticino, 522 of them being German.

At the same time that they are hosts to the world, the Swiss themselves have been restless peregrinators. Citizens of a claustrophobic little land, they seem to have bred into them the wanderlust of the country's 16th Century's mercenary soldiers. In 1607 some Bernese helped the English to settle Jamestown in Virginia. By 1750 several thousand Swiss had settled around Lancaster, Pennsylvania, becoming part of the group known as the "Pennsylvania Dutch." One of them, Albert Gallatin, served Presidents Jefferson and Madison as Secretary of the Treasury (characteristically Swiss, he reduced the national debt by 50 per cent). Later, John Sutter, a German-born Swiss, settled in California, and it was on his land that the gold was discovered which triggered the Gold Rush in 1848. Immigrants from the Ticino set up the California wine industry.

Other Swiss who made their names in the United States were the hotelkeeping brothers John and Peter Delmonico. Oscar Tschirky became known as Oscar of the Waldorf and was for years America's most famous maître d'hôtel. Of the many Swiss scientists working in America today, the best known is the California Institute of Technology's rocket physicist Fritz Zwicky.

IT is estimated that one tenth of the Swiss population is always living outside of Switzerland. Thousands of Swiss girls go to England each year and work as "mother's help" to learn the English language. As many young men go to the United States to serve their apprenticeship in American business. But probably the most curious example of all Switzerland's human give-and-take is the chorus of Wisconsin yodelers, some of them fourth-generation Americans of Swiss descent, who recently made a well-publicized concert tour of Switzerland, showing the old country what Swiss yodeling is really like.

The first men to succeed in a winter assault on the treacherous north wall of the Eiger reach the top after a seven-day ascent in 1961.

Impeccable Service in a Refreshing Atmosphere

Just as the lure of the great peaks has for centuries drawn men to Switzerland's mountain airs, so has the Swiss ability to look after guests been maintained on a high plane. The country has long prided itself in its tradition of hospitality. Making others feel at home is an art which requires attention to detail and perspicacious planning. Foreigners who visit briefly as tourists, skiing at mountain resorts or resting at spas, find their hotel accommodations comfortable, clean and reasonably priced—and the service impeccable. Those who come as students discover that Swiss training provides them—whether prospective hotel manager or next year's ski champion—with just the proficiency and confidence that they will require.

EFFERVESCENT PARTY of ski enthusiasts in Wolfgang, a small village in the Parsenn, one of Switzerland's famous skiing areas, is given a boost by champagne chilled in the snow.

CRISSCROSS TRAILS mark the nearly vertical Gotschnawang, a slope in the Parsenn, through snow dangerously close to avalanching. The Parsenn also has many easier runs for novices.

A FINISHING SCHOOL brings *intellectual stimulation and polish to girls from many lands*

SUPPER of French cuisine is a poised and sophisticated affair, served beautifully. Although students come from 22 countries, the official language at meals and in class is always French.

CONVERSATION with fellow students fills free time in the well-trimmed gardens adjoining La Châtelainie, an international institute in Neuchâtel for 136 girls from the ages of 14 to 20.

LIBRARY provides a quiet place for students to discuss French grammar with their teacher *(right)*. The school gives emphasis to the humanities, arts and sports as well as to the social graces.

BEDROOM affords a light and cheery place for Germaine Lecoeur, a 17-year-old French girl, to correct her homework before class. Scholastic programs are suited to a student's needs.

SMALL CLASS is characteristic of La Châtelainie in that it allows for individual attention from instructors. With a staff of about 50, there is a ratio of one teacher to every three girls.

ATTENTIVE APPRENTICE, a German girl watches a chef make the soup of the day at the Ecole Hôtelière in Lausanne, the oldest hotel school of its kind in the world.

CULINARY DEMONSTRATION absorbs students in the famous cuisine course. A student can take consecutive courses in service, cuisine (cooking) and administration.

A HOTEL SCHOOL teaches the fine points of the trade to fledgling chefs, waiters and managers from 23 countries

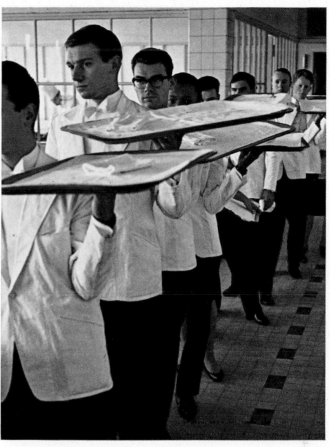

UNRUFFLED DEPORTMENT is acquired by students during the training in service. The entire curriculum at the Ecole Hôtelière takes 17 months and costs about $2,400.

MODEL LUNCH of hare stew *forestière* served to fellow students gives chefs and waiters an opportunity to put theory into practice. Graduates staff hotels throughout the world.

FINE HOTELS have won themselves a reputation for comfort and elegance

FASHIONABLE SPA on the Rhine, Bad Ragaz has several superlative hotels like the Quellenhof *(opposite)*. The photograph, made through the hotel windows, shows diners at their tables and also catches the outline of mountains reflected in the glass.

LUXURY ESTABLISHMENT, the Dolder Grand Hotel in Zurich provides tea and quiet surroundings *(right)* for guests who play cards. Zurich has more than 250 listed hotels and pensions; the most expensive single room is about $12 a night.

8

Enduring Ties with the Land

LITTLE herd boys lie on their backs or their bellies and their tiny white goats spring about on the mountain slopes," wrote short-story writer Katherine Mansfield during an Alpine journey. "You meet tiny girls all alone with flocks of black sheep or herds of huge yellow cows."

This idyllic, pastoral image of Switzerland, which is, in fact, one of the world's most intensely industrialized countries, is cherished not only by foreigners but by the Swiss themselves. Whether he is engaged in agriculture or not, a Swiss feels himself attached to the soil. No matter where he lives, he identifies with the canton where he was born, or with that fragment of land which his ancestors cultivated. He believes that the welfare of both man and nation is influenced not only by conditions of world economy but by the cycles of nature and the fertility of the earth.

Switzerland's 15,951 square miles can be divided into four portions of approximately equal acreage: lakes and barren rock, forests, grazing pastures and cultivated land. Most of the cultivated land is in the fertile plateau, 150 miles long and sometimes 30 miles wide, which rolls from the Jura Mountains to the Alps. This plateau is somewhat more than a quarter of the area of Switzerland. It is the area of fairy-tale villages, prosperous-looking farms with big brown barns, fields of grain, herds of fat cattle and, on the pine-forested Jura slopes, droves of horses.

It is the high-altitude areas devoted to grazing cattle, however, that have given the world its idyllic image of Switzerland. Dairy farming is the dominant way of life on the green highland meadows of the three original cantons of the Innerschweiz, of Bern, Valais and the Grisons, and of the rugged northeastern cantons of Glarus and Appenzell. Over one half of the area in Switzerland devoted to forestry lies in the same cantons. The combination of pasturing and forestry is responsible for the uninterrupted green color which has impressed visitors to Switzerland for centuries.

In the Middle Ages, many of the pastures were cultivated. But tillage of the steep slopes was an arduous, unfruitful task, and erosion washed away the plowed topsoil. In the 13th and 14th Centuries the mountaineers discovered that their thin lands were better suited to cattle raising and dairy farming. The science of cheese making made it possible to transform perishable milk into durable cheeses which could be kept for long periods and transported to urban markets, and the mountain people turned into dedicated dairymen. An 18th Century traveler to Switzerland found that in the highlands, "everything seems to be created for the cattle, and everything is subordinated to their needs and comforts; humans come only in second place."

THE cow came to be almost deified by the Swiss. The lonely Swiss herdsman, inarticulate with humans, feels a strong emotion for his cattle; if he is pious he may fall to his knees in his barn and thank God for his cows. In Appenzell, Schwyz and other cantons, cows are garlanded with flowers and serenaded with music before they begin their seasonal migrations up and down the Alps between their winter barns and their high summer pastures. Such loving attention, combined with careful breeding and feeding, has greatly improved the quality of Swiss cows over the centuries. The rugged half-wild little beasts of the early Middle Ages weighed 650 pounds; today Swiss cows are double that weight. A hundred years ago Switzerland had 500,000 cows; although the pasture area has been reduced by industrialization, today there are 1,716,000.

THERE are several breeds of cattle in Switzerland and a cattleman can tell what part of the country he is in by the color of the cows. The beige-tan ones, known as "Brown Swiss," graze in the pastures of eastern and central Switzerland. In the western cantons there are the white- and tawny-spotted Simmental breed; in Fribourg cows are black-and-white, and in the Valais there are fierce-looking brownish-black Eringer cows, one of the oldest cattle breeds in the world. The sounds of their bells, ranging from tiny treble tinkles to deep basso pealings, are the same all over Switzerland. Often old and elaborately fashioned, the bells help herdsmen to locate any cows that have wandered astray.

As cows are a symbol of Switzerland, so is cheese. The 31,000 tons of cheese exported each year are a small item in the Swiss economy, yet Swiss cheese, even more famous than Swiss watches, is the first product associated with the country.

The type of cheese known as "Swiss" in the world market is Emmentaler, first made in the valley of the Emme in the canton of Bern 400 years ago. This "king of cheeses" is prepared in golden wheels weighing as much as 260 pounds each, and has a mild, nutlike flavor. Today it is produced in 1,600 dairies in the lowlands of the German-speaking cantons.

Similar to Emmentaler but much more ancient, dating from the 12th Century, is Gruyère, made in the cantons of Fribourg, Neuchâtel, Vaud and in the Jura Mountains. Other varieties include Schabzieger, a green cheese from Glarus; Sbrinz, made in central Switzerland; Räss from Appenzell; Saanen, which has been known to last 100 years, from the canton of

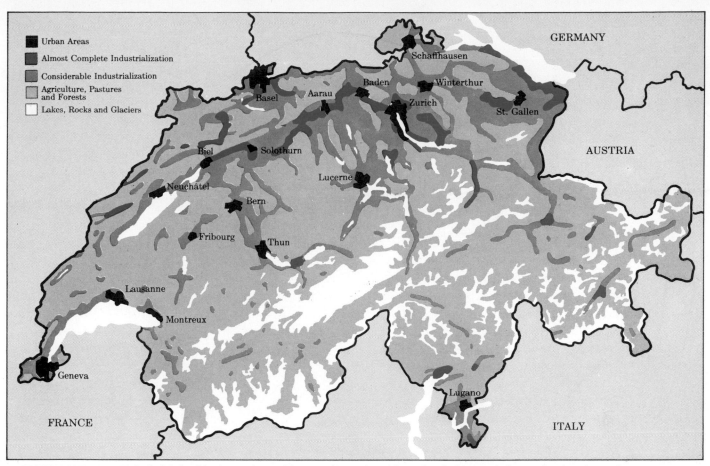

Legend:
- Urban Areas
- Almost Complete Industrialization
- Considerable Industrialization
- Agriculture, Pastures and Forests
- Lakes, Rocks and Glaciers

GERMANY
AUSTRIA
ITALY
FRANCE

Schaffhausen
Baden · Winterthur
Basel · Aarau · Zurich · St. Gallen
Biel · Solothurn
Neuchâtel · Bern · Lucerne
Fribourg · Thun
Lausanne
Montreux
Geneva
Lugano

HOW THE LAND IS USED in Switzerland is shown above. Although the country is highly industrialized, the regions given over to industry and manufacturing tend to be concentrated in the north, with much of the remainder predominantly rural and the rest *(white areas)* of marginal economic use. There are isolated industrial areas, however, throughout the country.

Bern; Vacherin from Fribourg; Tête de Moine from the Bernese Jura; Toggenburger from St. Gall; and Piora from the Ticino. Some Swiss cheeses are manufactured in the U.S. by exactly the same processes as in Switzerland, but the American versions lack the original flavors which come from the Alpine herbs that the cows eat on the high pastures during the milk-producing summer months.

The Swiss are never impractical romantics; their dedication to land and cows is born of an urgent expediency. The more Switzerland can produce from its own soil, the less the country is dependent on imported food. Today the country's cultivated land supports only about three fifths of the population. During World War II when marginal lands, flower gardens and even city parks were put under cultivation, production was increased, but still the Swiss people suffered from stringent food rationing.

The emergency brought farming back into the foreground and led to a recent Government drive to bring 741,000 acres permanently under the plow and insure a greater self-sufficiency when the flow of foodstuffs may again be interrupted. Agriculture, more than ever, has become a patriotic duty. Its political-economic urgency has made the farm problem in Switzerland even more critical than in most countries of the world. Of a total of 205,997 farms, more than half are 12 acres or less. Work on the hilly Swiss terrain is arduous, and the rewards are minimal. In a country which does not know deep poverty, the poorest classes include its hardest workers, the farmers. The older rural generation is stable and conservative, with the ancient virtues—energy, thrift, independence and love of land—still strong in its blood.

But for the younger generation, such patriotic dedication is no longer enough. Drawn by the lure of higher earnings, shorter hours and a more diverting life, many youths are migrating to the industrial cities. During this century's era of industrial expansion, more than half of Switzerland's villages have declined in population, some as much as 50 per cent.

This has been especially true in the Innerschweiz and in the high-altitude canton of the Grisons. A typical Grisons village that appears to be vanishing is Luven ob Ilanz, which sits on a slope in the Lungnez valley. "We are a farming community and farming is in great crisis," says the minister of the town, Dr. Conradin Bonorand. "Our population was once 300. Now it is 150 and most of the men are gone during the work week. The old concepts of liberty and freedom, which are the blood heritage of our people, no longer inspire the young. The promise of more money and more free time draws them away."

The minister, a sober and dedicated man who graduated from the University of Zurich and is a historian specializing in the Reformation, occasionally accompanies visitors on a walk through his parish, a cluster of 58 dark, decaying houses huddled on the mountainside like lichens on a rock. Some houses stand empty. Most are neglected, and in an utterly un-Swiss manner, weeds seem to be growing everywhere. Old ladies peer curiously at visitors from behind curtained windows.

"My parish has no youth left," the minister continues. "We are mostly women and children. Young men who have been taught trades give them up for other work. One of our carpenters is a postman in Zurich. A baker who learned his trade in our village is a railroad worker in Chur. Farmers have to sell their cows and goats because there is no one to care for them. When a farmer dies or leaves, there is no one to buy his farm and it stands abandoned."

TWO MEANINGS OF "ALP"

The term "the Alps" is used, of course, to denote the range of mountains which stretches across south-central Europe. The term has another local meaning, however. The Swiss and their German-speaking neighbors use it to denote the high Alpine meadows where cattle are pastured in the summer. (French-speaking Swiss call them *alpages*.) In this chapter, Alps (with a capital "A") means the mountains and alps (small "a") means the pastures.

In an effort to preserve a healthy farming system and prolong the life of villages like Luven ob Ilanz, the Swiss Government in 1951 passed an agriculture act which specifies that the earnings of a man working on the land should be equal to those of a man working in a factory. To bring this about, the Government controls prices on meat and dairy products and buys surpluses. In the case of bread grains, the Government simply buys the entire lot at double the world price. Quite apart from the price-raising effect of such a program on the Swiss housewife—the milk price is about 30 per cent above the average in Common Market countries, and the price of butter, 100 per cent—the agricultural program is costing Switzerland about $60 million a year.

In some areas the program is showing a beneficial effect. In the Valais, where the peasants are deeply attached to the land, this program, aided by a Government-sponsored plan to decentralize industry, has made it possible for the people to continue to farm. In northeastern Switzerland, where the towns frequently have small plants which employ those not needed on the land, there is also little migration to the cities. In short, in villages where a comfortable standard of living has been maintained, the ties of the land and family still hold the young. The Government hopes that with the help of its farm program, and an assist from local industry, these ties will remain strong.

In the mountainous dairying areas the year follows a satisfying if arduous ritual. Each summer a portion of the citizens climb to the highland meadows with their cows and live there in the barns and dairying houses until autumn signals a return to the village. In some parts of the Valais whole populations make the migrations, and villages duplicate themselves at different altitudes. In the Lötschental, where most of those who accompany the cows to the upper villages are women, the parish priest occasionally climbs on a Sunday morning to a height of 6,500 feet to read Mass for the pastured maidens, and then descends for a Mass in the valley at noon. In most cantons it is the men who accompany the cows, and they leave the company of women behind for the summer. The Alpine pastures are called alps. There are about 10,800 in Switzerland—15 per cent are the common property of the communes and 85 per cent are owned by individual farmers or private corporations.

A TYPICAL commune where dairying still flourishes is the village of Elm, high on the slopes of the Piz Segnes in the canton of Glarus. While other Swiss villages have diminished in size, Elm has steadily maintained its population of 900. It has an industry, a factory which bottles mineral waters which come from native springs. But most of Elm's 150 families are farm families, and at least 70 of them are considered by local standards to be prosperous. One of the successful farmers is Jakob Kubli, who inherited a farm in the valley from his father and whose sons will inherit the land from him. Each May, with his two young sons and two herdsmen, he takes 40 cows up to the Mühlebach alp. The ascent, during which the cows graze in meadows along the way, takes three weeks and ends at 6,000 feet. Here men and cows remain for 12 summer weeks.

Sometimes there are weekend visitors, and it is a tradition on the alps to offer hospitality—fresh milk to drink, bread and cheese to eat and a bed in the hay. Practiced hikers climb Mühlebach alp in five hours, but two visitors from America chose to ride in a jeep which could climb two thirds of the way.

The jeep, driven by its owner's 18-year-old son, was a vintage 1949 model. It chugged sturdily up through pine forests, past waterfalls and past the huts and pastures which were the cows' stopping-off places. Finally the road disappeared completely and the old jeep crept snail-like over rocks and tree roots, skidding in

forest loam, emerging finally above the *baumgrenze*—the tree line—into a great saucer of green meadows encircled by snowy peaks. It was the end of the line for the jeep. From there the visitors proceeded on foot.

Although it was dusk below, on the heights the sun still shone, and the upward path led through bright fields of flowers—alpine roses, daisies, foxglove and a variety of gentians, deep blue ones hugging the earth and tall, yellow ones from the roots of which mountaineers make a formidable *schnaps*. The path followed a stream, and the sound of rushing waters filled the evening. Soon there was another sound, the ringing of bells echoing and re-echoing in the mountains like a Balinese gamelan band. On the horizon ahead was a *stall*, a single low barn. The scene was like an illustration for *Heidi*. Sitting on benches were boys and bearded old men smoking long, curved pipes.

The barn housed cows, goats, men and a dairy. Two broad-shouldered young brothers named Willi and Fritz Landolt were milking cows. They said the Kubli *stall* was another two kilometers up the valley. After a rest the travelers continued on their way. The path led past ruins of barns crushed by avalanches. Finally a lamplight was seen flickering ahead, and out of the darkness emerged the shapes of two buildings, a *stall* and a *hütte*, or dairying hut. The buildings, newly built of gray stone, followed the contour of the mountain to withstand the winter avalanches that could roll over them. Both barn and hut were divided into halves, half of each operated by a farmer named Weber and half by Jakob Kubli.

T HOUGH it was almost 10 o'clock and bitterly cold, men and boys were still milking and making cheese. Jakob Kubli turned out to be a slightly built but muscular man, 49 years old. His sons Jakob, 15, and Heinrich, 13, were small, handsome lads who, in the manner of slow-maturing Alpine people, looked more like 12 and 10. They were dressed alike in wool shirts, heavy trousers held up by suspenders, and rubber boots, and they loped with bent shoulders in the curious Glarner gait which comes from carrying everlasting burdens. Silent, busy as gnomes, they were cooking whey to feed some pigs which were grunting at the door. The father said an older son, Rudi, was at home in the valley helping the mother harvest hay for winter fodder.

The hut was the center of a peaceable kingdom of men, pigs, goats, a horse and a herd of great matriarchal brown cows which, after they were milked, went off in a clangor of bells to graze in the meadows. A pungent odor of cooking milk, curing cheese and manure surrounded the place. Inside the hut was a cheese factory containing a great copper kettle of simmering milk, a stove, a cheese press and a rough board table.

WHEN the cows had been milked and the pigs fed, the two herdsmen who work for Jakob Kubli arrived from the barn. One of them, Jakob Rhyner, was a tall, thin fellow in his 20s with a wispy beard and long black curls. The other, Heinrich Hefti, about 50, had a dark leathery skin and grizzled beard, and he wore gold earrings in his pierced ears. After a scrubbing of milk buckets and a general washing-up, preparations for supper were begun. The two boys heated a saucepan of fresh milk and the herdsman, Rhyner, prepared a kettle of macaroni into which he chopped an onion. While the food cooked, the father lifted four new cheeses from their frames. They weighed about 44 pounds each and were soft and pliable, shining in the low light like flat, pale moons.

It was after midnight when supper and the last chores were finally finished. Outside, the cold night glittered with a million stars, and the mountains rang with bells. The father, carrying the lamp, led his sons and the herdsmen and guests up the stairs to sleep. Fully dressed, they squeezed together like sheep in a box of hay. Jakob and Rhyner lay smoking their pipes. The coals glowing so near the hay made the guests nervous, but Jakob assured them that the metal caps on the pipes made

smoking perfectly safe, that he smoked himself to sleep every night and picked the pipe out of the hay in the morning. At some time in the night the visitors were awakened by a boy's voice shouting, "Don't let them out! Don't let them out!" The father explained that the young Jakob often talked in his sleep, that he was herding cattle in his dreams.

In the morning the visitors woke up to a shivaree of bells. Though it was not yet 5 o'clock, they were alone in the hay. They got up, shook the hay out of their clothing and hair, and went downstairs where Rhyner was eating his breakfast, a bowl of coffee-milk and bread and cheese. It was Rhyner's job to herd 120 head of young cattle grazing another 1,300 feet up, just below the summit of the mountain, where he joined them each dawn. Into a rucksack of untanned cowhide he was packing lunch—bread, cheese and sausages. Outside, the pigs were feeding from their trough. The sun, a fiery red ball, was shining through a notch in the mountains.

"That's where I go, where the sun is," said Rhyner. From his aerie he boasted he could see Lake Constance, 47 miles to the north. Softly whistling *Lili Marlene,* he started to climb, a lean silhouette in the blinding glow. With his wide-brimmed hat at a rakish angle, the rucksack on his shoulders and a staff in his hand, he looked like an elongated young Don Quixote painted by El Greco. A horseless cowboy, he preferred, like his lonely breed the world over, solitude and the company of animals to human society.

IN the barn the Kubli boys and Heinrich Hefti were milking. The father carried the milk into the hut 90 liters at a time, staggering under the curved metal bucket strapped to his shoulders, emptying it into the cheese-making kettle without spilling a drop by twisting his body to one side. On each trip he asked his guests some new question about America. Did they know his uncle, Werner, who had emigrated 50 years ago? Was it true that all cows in America were milked by machines?

He said he had heard America was a land where women controlled everything, even *den geldsack*. No self-respecting man could bear a woman controlling his purse strings, he said, and he supposed that his unmarried guests had come to Switzerland to seek Swiss wives. Jakob admitted he would like to go to America to visit his cousins, but he doubted he ever could —it would be necessary to sell all his cows to make the trip, he said.

It was 9 o'clock when the milking was finished. The sun had warmed the high meadows and the visitors removed some of their sweaters. In the hut the father was stirring rennet into the kettle of milk to curdle it, beginning the cheese-making process. His younger son, Heinrich, boiled a mixture of coffee and milk. While they breakfasted, the father told of the old days when 50 farmers made the summer migration. Now there were only 16, he said. He remembered, as a boy, herds of a thousand goats. Now there were only a handful. In the old days farmers made hay on the alps and carried it halfway down on their shoulders, hauling it the rest of the way on sleds. A sled was still used, even in the snowless summers, to haul the cheeses home. Pulling it was the work of the horse that grazed with the cows. On the steep downhill slopes of the alps wheels were useless.

AT about 10 o'clock a group of Sunday Alpinists arrived, carrying bouquets of alpine roses. One climber, who had already scaled the mountain, brought the news that there was a sick calf on the summit. A rescue party was quickly organized to bring it down. The Americans joined the posse; so did an Alpinist in his 50s named Hans Hämmerli, who had climbed the Mühlebach alp for sport. The party followed a stream, wading part of the way upward in its bed. The mountains seemed covered with Sunday visitors, calling to one another in the curiously bloodcurdling shriek the Swiss use at high altitudes. The goal of the rescuers was the notch through which the sun had risen, the mountain pass where the herdsman, Rhyner,

spent his days. High above, silhouetted against the heavens, was a line of cows moving along the crest of the mountain.

Rhyner was nowhere to be found. The men shouted his name, but the only responses were the echoes of their voices and the clatter of cowbells. Finally a boy found the herdsman taking a nap in the lee of a rock. Aroused, Rhyner blinked dazedly at the men surrounding him, got up, adjusted his hat on his head and led them to the sick calf.

WHEN the men had departed with the animal, carrying it over the snows and precipices, Rhyner returned to his flower-upholstered bed. On the horizon was a seemingly endless procession of glacier-topped peaks; below were the green, rolling meadows. It was a place to remember the words with which de Saussure, the first great Alpinist, described his sensations when he finally reached the summit of Mont Blanc: "It seemed that I alone had survived the Universe. . . ."

As the rescue party arrived at the hut with the calf, the Kubli boys ran out with binoculars, eager to show the returning visitors a chamois. The graceful animal was perched on a distant crag, looking exactly as it does in pictures or in wood carvings, thin-legged, alert, with short, curving horns. It stayed a long time on its rock, surveying the valleys below, and then, as if suddenly aware of watching eyes, leaped from its lookout and disappeared.

In the hut, four new white cheeses were forming in the molds. It was mid-Sunday, the only time in the week when the flow of work was interrupted. Jakob was boiling a soft hot pudding of cream, flour and sugar which is a specialty of the Alps. A bottle of the gentian *schnaps* was set on the table. During the meal Jakob Kubli explained the economy of his summer operation. The alp, he said, belonged to the commune, from which he rented it. Half of the 40 cows he milked were his own; the others were on loan from neighbors down in the valley. For their care he was entitled to 180 francs' worth (about $42) of milk per cow per summer. For any milk over the 180-franc limit he paid the owners of the cows.

Snow falls several times each summer on the alp, but it quickly melts in the sun. About September 10, when the snows become frequent and the weather turns cold, the descent into the valley begins. The caravan stops at an alp called Gams, a third of the way down, and after 10 days there moves to a still lower alp called the Ublital. Finally, about October 1, men and cows reach Elm and home.

Heinrich, the younger boy, considered it a misfortune that he would have to descend three weeks before the others to begin school. His brother was happy to be finished with school. Neither the boys nor their father had ever seen a motion picture. The family had made one visit to Zurich by train to visit an aunt who lived there, but the boys had not liked it and did not want to go again. "We're not accustomed to that kind of life," said young Jakob. "Everyone knows Elm is the nicest place in the world. Who would want to leave it?"

THE time had come for the guests to leave. Arrangements had been made for the jeep to meet them at the timber line. As they waved goodbye to the Kublis, they saw that the two boys were already herding cows in from the pasture for the evening milking.

The uncrowded houses of Elm stand in blazing gardens of geraniums, begonias, delphiniums and asters. On the austere white wall of the 500-year-old church is a tablet bearing the names of 114 persons who lost their lives when an avalanche covered half of the village in 1881. On the mountain above the town the black scar of the landslide is still visible. The names on the tablet—Elmer, Bäbler, Rhyner, Kubli—are the same as the names of families in Elm today.

There is no bathroom in the hotel in Elm, but the manager arranged for the guests from America to have baths in the new home of the local *baumeister,* or architect-builder, Kaspar Rhyner. The 32-year-old architect had recently moved back to his village from Zurich with

his wife and two children. His modern house had oil paintings, a library and a bar, where he served his guests Martini cocktails. Rhyner told them of his education at Zurich's Federal Institute of Technology, of six years spent working as a stonemason by day and attending classes at night. Afterwards he worked three years as a builder in Zurich. "But I always wanted to return to Elm," he said. "I never really considered anything else. My attitude is not an unusual one. The traditional Swiss ties with the ancestral soil still prevail here."

Rhyner credits the railroad, brought up to Elm in 1905, as being responsible for the town's survival. "Many of our people take the train each morning to work in factories down in the valley of Glarus. But the real backbone of Elm is still its farming families."

In their daily lives the farmers of Elm prefer the old ways. Hay is still carried partway down the mountains on the backs of men. Stored at a halfway point, it is rolled down to the barns over the snow in winter. There is no dentist in the valley and only one doctor, in the neighboring village of Matt. There are only 10 automobiles in the community. On the other hand, many farmers have tractors or jeeps bought with Government subsidies. The traditional diet of bread, meat and cheese has been improved by deep-freeze lockers and by a vegetable truck which visits Elm once a week in winter.

THERE is also a pub in Elm, a lively place called Die Sonne. There, on that Sunday night, young men and girls danced polkas, and at tables against the walls men and women played *Jass,* the Swiss game of cards. A storm was moving down from the mountains. Suddenly an alarm spread through the village: A middle-aged woman who had wandered alone into the mountains that afternoon had not returned. A volunteer party of rescuers was organized. The Americans, who had helped rescue a calf in the morning, now joined the search for the lost lady. No one slept until the word was spread before midnight that the lady had been found and brought home on a tractor.

Straining not to spill a drop, Jakob Kubli bends his torso as he pours milk from a can strapped to his back into a cheese-making vat.

A Life of Hard Work in the High Alpine Pastures

Summer in rural Switzerland sees one of the world's most curious migrations. At the end of May, the farmers herd their cattle from the valley meadows and village barns to fresh pastures thousands of feet up in the Alps. There men and cattle live for three months or more until chill autumn winds drive them down into the valleys once more. On this and the following pages, photographs by Farrell Grehan evoke the hard—but in many ways idyllic—life of farmer Jakob Kubli, his sons and his herdsmen as they care for the cows and make cheese in their summer farm buildings high in the mountains above their native village of Elm.

CLEANING A PAIL, young Jakob Kubli, farmer Kubli's 15-year-old son, prepares to milk the cows, a one-legged milking stool strapped around his waist.

CARRYING MILK on his back in a 90-liter can, farmer Kubli crosses the neat farmyard from the slant-roofed barn, which follows the mountain slope.

MAKING THE CHEESE, Kubli adds milk which has ripened overnight to a kettle full of fresh milk. The cheese-making gear is in a stone *hütte*.

REMOVING THE CHEESECLOTH from a freshly pressed cheese, Kubli's neighbor prepares to set it in a salt bath. Later it will be stored on a shelf.

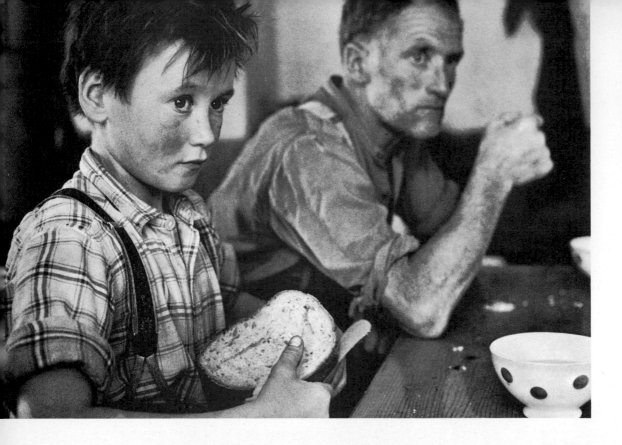

Herdsman Heinrich Hefti, who helps the Kublis tend their cows, enjoys a smoke before going to sleep next to one of the young boys in the haylo[ft]

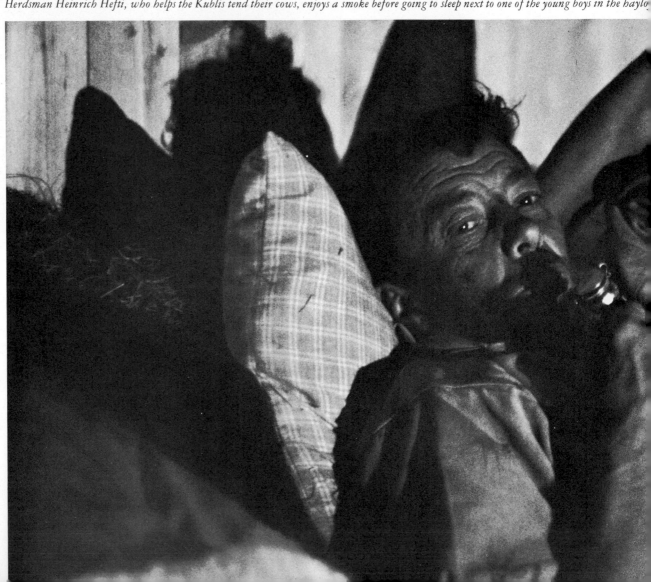

ver the "hütte." Like many Swiss mountain men, Hefti wears gold earrings. Everyone works until after midnight, and all arise at 5 a.m.

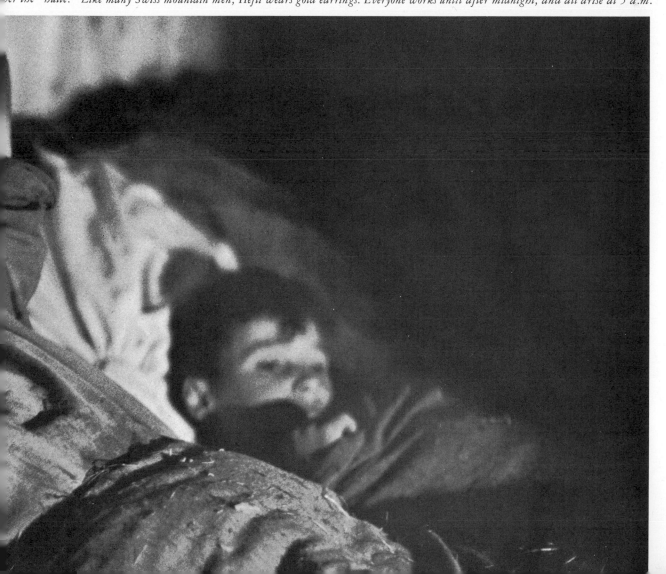

MORNING CHORES occupy the Kubli boys *(left)* as Heinrich washes a pot and Jakob whittles kindling to make it burn more readily. The boys do a multitude of jobs as they learn by experience to run a farm as efficiently as does their father.

TIMELESS SCENE reminiscent of rural paintings of the Dutch School is re-created by young Jakob *(opposite)* as he milks a fat and placid cow under the beamed roof of the *stall*. The *stall* has a sloping roof to help it withstand winter avalanches.

CHILDREN'S DUTIES include tending fires and making breakfast *(below)*. Jakob pours steaming coffee into a pot as he readies a meal for the farmers. Heinrich sees to it that the fire which heats the cheese-making vat is burning properly.

9

Espionage and Intrigue

TO the writer of thrillers, says Ian Fleming, creator of the now famous secret agent James Bond, Switzerland offers great temptations. A number of the most notable writers of tales of international intrigue have been unable to resist the lure. Somerset Maugham's suave and very British World War I spy, Ashenden, made his headquarters in a Geneva hotel which was chockablock with wily Orientals, overripe countesses and other threatening figures doubtless in the secret employ of the Central Powers. Joseph Conrad's brilliant, though little-read, spy novel, *Under Western Eyes*, takes place largely on Geneva's boulevards. Indeed, it is a rare

writer of thrillers who has not had at least one hero searched by Swiss border guards, shadowed through the streets of Bern, slugged in Zurich or drugged in Geneva, and then spirited by The Enemy to a remote Alpine chalet.

The curious part about all this fiction is that it comes very close to being fact. Without question, neutral little Switzerland is one of the most spy-infested countries in the world. More than one tenth of the people living in Switzerland today are foreigners, and while the efficient Swiss police do not think that all of them are potential secret agents, it is accepted that the number of spies in the country runs into the thousands. During both world wars Switzerland was undoubtedly the leading collection point of Europe's secret intelligence.

The advantages that Switzerland offers secret agents are considerable. The Swiss are tolerant of foreigners and refugees, and there are so many of them in Switzerland that they go relatively unnoticed. Then there is the central location: Berlin, Rome, Paris and Vienna are all less than a day away by train. Switzerland's banks, in which accounts may be secret and anonymous, provide an international cashier's office for the easy and confidential transmission of monies. In addition, Switzerland has three international cities which are the natural clearinghouses for the world's mercantile and diplomatic intelligence—the political capital of Bern, the commercial and banking center of Zurich, and the seat of international conferences and offices, Geneva. Perhaps the most striking advantage of all has been Switzerland's tradition of political neutrality. The Swiss are not officially hostile to anyone, and captured spies are seldom shot, even in wartime, but are merely jailed or deported. For the proliferation of spies, such a climate is just about perfect.

IF the Swiss seem to be calm spectators at the never-ending cloak-and-dagger drama for which they provide the stage, it is because Switzerland's role has been less that of an actual target of spies than of a crossroads for people spying on the country's neighbors. Even as late as the 1930s, a minimum of spying activities was directed against Switzerland itself. There was not much to spy on, even during World War I, in either Swiss diplomacy or defense, nor were there any important war industries. In 1916 two Swiss Army colonels named Karl Egli and Moritz von Wattenwyl were court-martialed for passing information to Germany about Allied troop movements, but Swiss indignation was aroused not so much by the fact that the information had been passed as by the officers' betrayal of Swiss neutrality. Most foreign agents caught spying then as now were simply expelled from the country.

The casual attitude about espionage came to an end in the mid-1930s when the Swiss became aware that Russian and German agents were abducting people who had sought refuge in Switzerland from Hitler or Stalin. The shocked Swiss Government passed a law in 1936 which made espionage a criminal offense even when no Swiss person or interests were involved. Swiss persons and interests soon did become vitally involved. By 1938 the country suddenly seemed filled with Hitler's agents and sympathizers. Almost half of the 400,000 foreigners then in Switzerland were Germans. Many Nazi diplomats, it developed, were either spies or propagandists or both. There were 66 organized Nazi Party and Hitler youth groups with a membership of over 5,000. German radio transmitters, as well as caches of TNT, were discovered. Switzerland itself had plainly become a target of espionage and subversion.

With the outbreak of World War II, Switzerland became the center of wholesale espionage operations, with literally thousands of agents operating throughout the country. Most of them were either Allied agents using Switzerland as a base for intelligence operations against Germany and Italy or German and Italian agents seeking information about Allied military movements. But a certain amount of spying this time was directed against Switzerland. Both to protect their own nation and to aid the Allies, Swiss counterintelligence forces smoked out and arrested hundreds of agents employed by Germany and Italy.

WORLD WAR II also saw the emergence of a powerful Swiss intelligence apparatus. During and after the Nazi invasion of Poland, Hitler had given frequent assurances that Swiss neutrality would not be violated. But some men who had seen Swiss intelligence reports were not deceived. They suspected not only that their country was part of Hitler's design for a Greater Germany but also that an invasion across the Rhine was already contemplated by the German general staff. One of the men who doubted Hitler's protestations of friendship was Henri Guisan, who became the commanding general of the Swiss Army on the critical date of August 30, 1939.

The 65-year-old soldier had retired to his farm in the canton of Vaud when Parliament called on him to head Switzerland's defense. On the next day, the Swiss Government announced that Switzerland would defend itself against any armed attack. On September 1, when the German invasion of Poland began, Guisan ordered mobilization of the entire able-bodied male population, thereby putting one fourth of Switzerland's men under arms. Across the Rhine the *Führer* understood that the shrewd old Swiss warrior meant business.

AFTER the fall of Poland, Guisan and his advisers became increasingly aware that the German leader was no ordinary bellicose neighbor but a murderous fanatic bent on conquering all of Europe. If he succeeded, they knew, Switzerland would be at Hitler's mercy. This was no time for strict adherence to Switzerland's traditional form of neutrality. Guisan and his general staff determined to do all they could, short of precipitating an invasion by any of the belligerent powers, to aid the Allies and fight the German monster.

Guisan's most useful weapon was his "ND," or *Nachrichten-Dienst*, the Swiss Army's Information Service, and its affiliated and highly secret intelligence agency, the "Bureau Ha." Enlarging these operations, the general turned espionage into a successful tool of foreign policy and a strategy of war. Throughout the terrible five and a half years it took to defeat Hitler, Guisan's intelligence men supplied the Allies with countless pieces of valuable information. Unfortunately not all of this information fell on receptive ears, especially at first.

In the early spring of 1940, through information received by their intelligence agencies, the Swiss were able to warn the Allies that Hitler was planning to invade Denmark, Norway, Holland and France. The Allied chiefs of staff regarded the Swiss information as being far too alarmist. Shortly after receiving it, Prime Minister Neville Chamberlain told a Conservative Party conference that "Hitler has missed the bus." Denmark, Norway, Holland and France all ignored the Swiss warnings. It may well be that if the Swiss information had been acted upon in time, the disasters which overtook these countries could have been averted.

While such information was being ignored by the Allies, Guisan's policy of refusing to accommodate the Nazis was being opposed by some members of the federal Government and a segment of the Swiss population which still believed Swiss survival would best be served by not unduly antagonizing Germany. France's capitulation in June 1940, however, shocked the nation into a realization of the nature of the Nazi menace. Then, on July 25, Guisan rallied his staff on Switzerland's hallowed Rütli meadow. Arriving by boat across the Lake of Lucerne, the general, in a dramatic appeal for national solidarity, outlined a program for turning Swiss neutrality into a practical instrument for defending Swiss independence. He told the assembled officers that Switzerland had to resist all attacks and pressures from the outside as well as from defeatists within Switzerland. "We are at the turning point of our history," he said. "The existence of Switzerland is at stake."

The meeting on the Rütli made patriotic Swiss aware of the need for unity. Though a few members of the Government still refused to accept the fact that a resistance movement had begun, the Swiss people had found in Guisan a new national leader to add to their long roster of strong military heroes. Neutrality remained the country's official policy, but the Swiss Army was in effect at war.

THE powerful Bureau Ha, which operated from a villa on the Lake of Lucerne, established agents in Rome, Paris and Helsinki and strengthened its "Viking Line" to Berlin, penetrating right into the Nazi high command. Using these agents to plant as well as harvest information, Guisan let it be known that his Army engineers had mined the St. Gotthard and Simplon tunnels as well as other essential communications links and that they would be destroyed the moment Switzerland was invaded. This, with a later threat to virtually demolish all Swiss industry in the event of an attack, is credited with convincing Hitler that an invasion of Switzerland would be folly. Swiss intelligence continued to share its information with the Allies, and was certainly one of the most knowledgeable and effective espionage agencies operating during the war.

In 1942 a new face appeared on the stage of Swiss intrigue when Allen W. Dulles arrived in Bern to take charge of an important overseas branch of the U.S. Office of Strategic Services. Recognizing the exceptional abilities of Swiss Army intelligence—and the past failures of the Allies to exploit its services—Dulles worked closely with Guisan. They saw to it that the ND's superior intelligence was shared not only with the Americans in Bern but also with French and British agents in Zurich. Relevant portions of the information unearthed by the spies of all these nations were also shared, albeit indirectly and unofficially, with agents of the Soviet Union in Geneva.

Up to the time of Hitler's attack on Poland, Soviet intelligence operations in Switzerland had been negligible. No official Soviet diplomatic personnel had been in Switzerland since relations between Bern and Moscow had been broken off in 1923. In the 1930s a few Soviet agents settled in Switzerland, among them two women known as Vera and Sonia, as well as men using women's names. One of these, called "Dora," a mild-mannered Hungarian whose real name was Alexander Rado, became the center of a large Soviet intelligence network in Switzerland after 1939. Rado posed as an innocent geographer who published maps.

AS director in Switzerland of the *Rote Kapelle* (often translated as Red Choir), which was the code name for Soviet intelligence in Western Europe, Rado sometimes had 50 agents working for him. His second in command and chief radio operator, an Englishman named Alexander Foote, later admitted to

sending 6,000 messages to Moscow before the Swiss civil police—who, unlike the military police, refused to tolerate Russian espionage—routed the *Rote Kapelle* in 1943. In bad odor with their employers, "Dora" and Foote were summoned to Moscow in 1945. "Dora" was probably executed. Foote was absolved and eventually escaped to England.

THE spy who supplied Rado and his *Rote Kapelle* with most of their intelligence was the legendary "Lucy," perhaps the most successful master spy of modern times. The true identity of "Lucy" was not known during the war either to "her" Soviet employers or to the U.S. intelligence director, Allen Dulles.

Actually, "Lucy"—so named because "she" operated from Lucerne—was a middle-aged, thick-spectacled man undistinguished enough in appearance to be mistaken for a bank teller or a hotel concierge. His name was Rudolf Rössler, and he was a German who had been a theatrical producer in Berlin and the editor of an anti-Nazi newspaper in Bavaria. When Hitler came to power in 1933, Rössler fled to Switzerland, where he worked as a correspondent on a newspaper and began a publishing firm.

Through a friend named Xavier Schnieper, who was an ND agent, Rössler in 1939 became a spy for the Swiss Army intelligence service. In taking this step Rössler seems to have been motivated solely by his violent hatred of the Nazis. His contacts in Berlin were so extensive and accurate that his employers sometimes distrusted what he reported, suspecting that he must be a counterspy. A month before the German attack on Russia, he predicted this event to the ND. The information was slipped to the *Rote Kapelle* and in 1942, Rössler, still moved by his anti-Nazi feelings, became an agent also for the Russians, filing the same reports to both Swiss and Russian channels.

Rössler went on to greater triumphs. His sources, although nobody knows exactly what they were, seem to have been on the highest levels. He so amazed his Russian accomplices with the completeness of his day-to-day reports of Nazi troop movements that they became convinced that such accurate intelligence could only come directly from Hitler's *Oberkommando*. Some scholars studying the Russian campaign today believe that information supplied by the mysterious "Lucy" was to a large extent responsible for the final defeat of the German *Wehrmacht* on the Eastern front.

Becoming more and more pro-Communist, Rössler continued to be a Communist agent after the war, conducting spying operations against West Germany on behalf of the Czechoslovakian secret service. In 1953 he and his friend Schnieper were arrested by the Swiss as spies. Rössler's lawyer, reminding the court of his client's wartime role, and of the fact that he had never spied against the Swiss, said, "Switzerland may have to rely on men like Rössler again in a new emergency." The court let Rössler off with a light sentence. He was allowed to stay in Switzerland, where he died in 1958.

THE end of "Lucy" did not noticeably lessen the amount of espionage being carried on in Switzerland. In a land where sensationalism is regarded as an unpatriotic vice, news about spy plots is usually compressed into 10-line press statements—just enough to show that Swiss counterespionage is operating with its customary precision despite the gradual postwar abolition of border checks and the automation of telephones which have made it harder to keep track of what suspected agents are up to. The periodic expulsion of Communist diplomats from the country indicates that Switzerland still is a clearinghouse for East-bound intelligence. At least 15 cases of espionage uncovered since 1954 have involved agents from Communist countries. Other cases involved two Swiss nationals arrested for spying for East Germany and two Israeli agents involved in an underground effort to keep German scientists out of Egypt's armament industry.

That Swiss counterintelligence agents have other things to worry about in addition to Communists was demonstrated by the country's most sensational postwar spy case, one which involved not the East but Algeria. In 1957 a pro-Algerian Frenchman who was an agent of France's secret service, the *Deuxième Bureau,* informed the Egyptian embassy in Bern that its telephone lines were being tapped and information was thus being obtained concerning Egypt's undercover support of the Algerian liberation movement. This damaging information, the agent said, was getting back to interested ears in Paris. The Egyptians complained about the wire tapping to the Swiss Foreign Minister, who began an investigation. The Associated Press thereupon broke the story that it was not French spies but Swiss counterintelligence agents who had been tapping the Egyptian embassy telephone lines.

The Swiss Minister of Justice summoned Switzerland's ablest spy-hunter, René Dubois, who as the country's Attorney General was director of the Swiss police and their counterintelligence agents, to discuss the rumors. After a conversation in the capitol building, the 48-year-old Attorney General was seen rushing through the streets of Bern toward his suburban flat, where he took out his Army pistol and shot himself. The next day the Swiss Government issued a communiqué which, in effect, admitted that the Attorney General had illegally furnished information to a foreign power.

News of the suicide provoked such public consternation as no living Swiss had ever seen. The staid *Neue Zürcher Zeitung* proclaimed it "the biggest scandal since our Confederation was founded," and other papers hinted ominously of corruption in Bern and a "crisis of confidence" in the Government.

IN the midst of such alarms, of spying and counterspying, it can never be easy to winnow rumor from fact. One thing, however, appears fairly certain. From General Guisan's change-over from passive to active neutrality there has been no road back. Already Switzerland's days of remote uninvolvement seem faded into history. Behind the serenely beautiful face of the land, behind the geranium boxes, the hidden turmoil is not likely to abate.

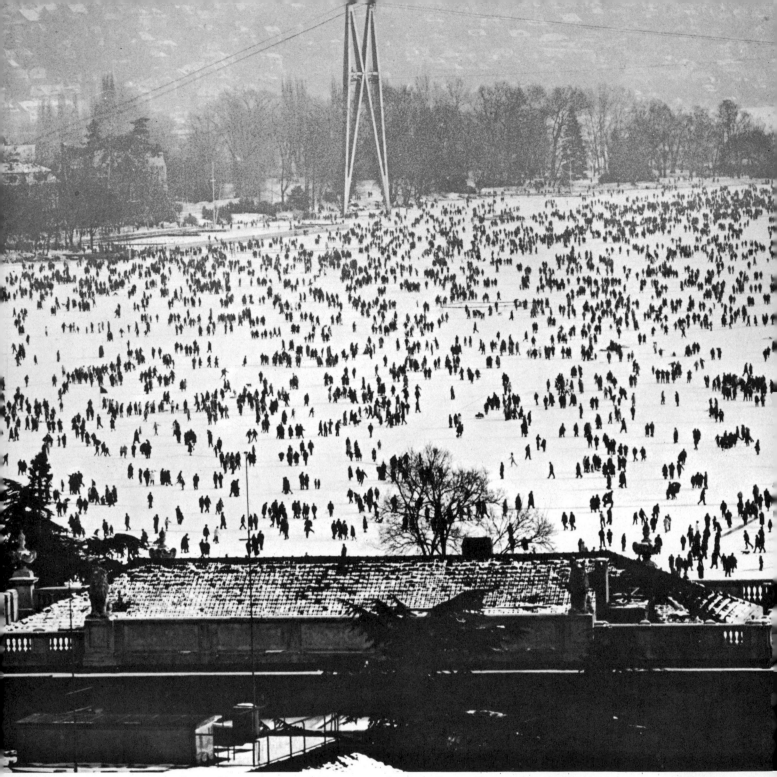

During a bitter cold snap, the worst of this century, in the winter of 1963, the Lake of Zurich froze over. Some 150,000 sportsmen donned

A Nation on
a Busman's Holiday

Natives of the "Playground of Europe," which devotes itself so thoroughly to accommodating foreign guests, the Swiss might be expected to turn to quiet pursuits in private moments. Surprisingly, they do nothing of the kind. In

boots or skates and took to the ice, presenting to the passing spectator a breathtaking view. The last time the lake froze over was in 1928.

their free time the Swiss ski instructors ski and the mountaineers climb. Fresh air and vigorous activity, natural concomitants of rural life, are more difficult for an urban population to obtain. Nevertheless, Switzerland's excellent network of roads and electric trains aid the city sportsman's exodus to the country, where he avidly pursues shooting, boating and camping. And, in typical Swiss fashion, an organization with a rule book governs every sport imaginable.

MOUNTAIN HIKE organized by the Boy Scouts passes through the little village of Melchthal in the canton of Unterwalden. Like their American counterparts, Swiss Boy Scouts spend their vacation holidays going on organized camping expeditions.

AWARD CEREMONY ending two days of competition in a national Swiss game called Hornussen draws a crowd of athletes and spectators. Hornussen involves two teams driving a wooden disk down a 300-yard-long course with long, flexible ashen clubs.

CAMPING SITE beside the Lake of Zug commands a view of the Rigi, the small peak rising in the background. Although the Rigi itself has long been a tourist's landmark, this part of the lakefront is not frequented by foreigners, and many Swiss vacation in the area. Switzerland has more than 400 supervised locations for camping, many of them with permanent facilities.

141

BALLOONING brings experts from nine countries to navigate in the high winds of the Bernese Alps

PREPARING FOR TAKEOFF, balloonists gather around their inflated but sandbagged craft before making final adjustments. Privately owned, the balloons fly the flags of each owner's country—the Swiss cross and the yellow, orange and black German tricolor. The first International Ballooning Week took place in 1962, the centennial of the first balloon-crossing of the Alps.

10

The Success of Thinking Small

FOR the 20th Century it was a curious sight. Seven beautiful young English women in the height of 19th Century fashion, wearing tiny Empress Eugénie hats, cashmere shawls and dresses with bishop's sleeves and petticoats which showed an occasional flash of frilled pantaloons, arrived in Geneva to make the Swiss Grand Tour. They were accompanied by six young Englishmen in fore-and-aft hats, tangerine weskits and sack coats.

They were guests of the Swiss Government, invited to re-enact the first Cook's Tour of Switzerland held exactly one century before. For 12 days they traveled by stagecoach, by steam trains resurrected from the Transportation Museum in Lucerne, by paddlewheel steamers and by foot and donkeyback. They dined on roast ox and read Byron in the Château de Chillon, breakfasted in neck-to-ankle bathing costumes and played chess from buoyant chessboards in the hot baths of Leukerbad. They rode over the snow-filled Gemmi Pass in Gemmi carriages, on which passengers faced the rear, their backs to the horse. They were carried on sedan chairs up the Rigi for the traditional sunrise viewing, and they were floated over the Alps in balloons. Wherever the visitors went, there were Swiss to greet them with flowers and music, food and wine. In Alpnachstad the world-champion crossbow marksman, a 35-year-old house painter named Xavier Schön, shot an arrow squarely through an apple at 40 paces, and at the lakeside village of St. Niklausen an old lady, her face tear-stained, grasped the hand of one of the Englishmen and said, "I was in London for Queen Victoria's funeral. Oh, those were beautiful days."

The ordinarily imperturbable Swiss are easily stirred by nostalgia for more leisurely times. Up in Elm, a grandmother, who as a girl barely escaped death in the great landslide of 1881, said sadly, "It used to be restful here in our village. But now it has become very dangerous. On Sundays an automobile goes by almost every half hour." Swiss dramatist Friedrich Dürrenmatt says, "We live with one foot in the past and the other in the modern age."

Nostalgia produces, along with a love of the past, a love of smallness. Suspecting things that are large in scope, the Swiss have made a success of thinking small. They have a habit of scaling everything down to minute size. Ringing through the Swiss-German language like perpetual baby chatter is the diminutive suffix *li*. *"Mir si z'fride mit üsem Ländli,"* a farmer says, *"üsne Bärgli u Küeli u üsne Schwyzer Fränkli. . . ."* ("We're satisfied with our little country, our little mountains and little cows, and the little Swiss francs. . . .")

NEITHER Swiss mountains nor cows are Lilliputian, and the Swiss franc is more substantial than most other currencies. But the Swiss go on making things small, until sometimes the whole country sounds almost like a kindergarten. The Mediterranean wife of a Zurich doctor describes the Swiss as "a nation of well-behaved mice." They are, she says, petits bourgeois, preoccupied with detail and tormented by an obsession for cleanliness.

The cult of diminution may be simply a result of the national inferiority complex. A Swiss psychologist says, "Our group inferiority—the inferiority of a small country in a big world—becomes each man's personal inferiority." C. F.

Ramuz, Switzerland's finest 20th Century writer and one of its sternest critics, wrote, "Rich in low things, poor in high things, [the Swiss] . . . might be considered worthy folk who don't interfere with others so that others should not interfere with them."

ALTHOUGH the Swiss make a point of not interfering with others, there is no denying the fact that they often find themselves involved in other people's business. They are easy and indefatigable travelers who sometimes appear to believe they are turning the Western world into an extension of Switzerland. Should the bomb ever devastate our globe, the Swiss believe they would still be there, safe in their natural bomb shelters in the deep valleys of Schwyz, Valais, Bern and the Grisons, ready to emerge and take over the scorched earth. There would be Swiss physicians, agriculturists, financiers, food experts and International Red Cross workers to roam over the desolate lands, filing reports, helping people to remake their lives and outlining plans for the rebuilding of the world on a firm Swiss business basis.

The Swiss involvement with the rest of the world has taken on new meaning in recent years. One of the problems it still has not solved is the squaring of its traditional policy of neutrality with present-day conditions. One of the men who helped to move the country into modern times was its wartime commander-in-chief, Henri Guisan. By persuading the Government to build military redoubts in the Alps, by running an efficient military intelligence network, and by threatening to dynamite the Gotthard and Simplon tunnels and other strategic links if Switzerland were invaded, the jaunty little general demonstrated for his people that neutrality and independence were no longer synonymous and that there was nothing heroic or noble in remaining uncommitted when one's ideological brothers are committed. With his wartime record he showed that neutrality can be a positive foreign policy instead of a negative, ostrichlike avoidance of any policy. Since World War II the Swiss have accepted this policy of neutral activism, which they acknowledge has become essential to the continued independence and defense of Switzerland.

Today the Swiss envision active neutrality in the context of the whole world. Experienced as hosts to East-West conferences and to myriad international offices, they now quickly reach out to mediate between countries that stop speaking to one another. The Swiss have stepped into the diplomatic breach between the United States and Cuba and have served on truce inspection committees in Korea. They have even established their own foreign-aid program, beginning with a 1961 grant of almost $14 million earmarked for giving technical assistance of all kinds to underdeveloped countries in Africa, Asia and Latin America. A humanity divided between a Communist East and a non-Communist West, between a rich industrial north and a poor agrarian south, between colored peoples and whites, is going to continue providing opportunities for intercession. A country which has no imperialistic ambitions and which has for centuries provoked not a single political enemy, will continue to qualify as the world's most responsible neutral.

ONE of Switzerland's most puzzling enigmas is the nation's extreme political conservatism. Living in something very much like a welfare state, the Swiss nonetheless look on Communism as the Devil's workshop. Swiss conservatism is the conservatism of the mountain peasant. In heart and in soul, Switzerland has not broken with the soil, and therein lies its durability. Today a quarter of the people live in the country's 10 largest towns, but they retain their rural character. City Swiss have not forgotten the challenge that their wild and rugged lands flung at generations of their ancestors, nor have they abandoned the thrift and tenaciousness with which their forefathers faced that challenge.

In spirit Switzerland looks West. A landlocked island bound by cultures, languages and ancestry to Germany, France and Italy, the country paradoxically feels itself closer to the Atlantic sphere of seafaring peoples—to the British and the Americans, to the Dutch and the Scandinavians—than to its hereditary kinsmen. The Swiss like to point out that one of the first English-language Bibles was published in Geneva in 1560; that their own Professor Jacob Burckhardt predicted in 1872 that English would be the future world language; that when Switzerland was threatened, as it was by Napoleon and Hitler, it was to Anglo-Saxon countries that it turned for friendship.

The bond is based partly on the powerful flow of religious and political ideas carried from Geneva to Britain, and thence to America by the *Mayflower* Pilgrims. As with the Constitutions of England, of the United States, of Norway and of Sweden, Switzerland's Constitution grew organically, in response to political experience. From a recognition of common interest and an easy, frequently English-speaking communication, there has grown binding trust and sympathy between these Protestant capitalist states. Because Switzerland needed no Marshall Plan aid, there also has been none of the resentment felt by a poor receiver for a rich donor. In no country in Europe has there been less response to postwar anti-American propaganda. In 1963 when England was rejected for membership in the Common Market, the indignant Swiss were almost relieved to remember that their own bid for associate membership had been shelved the previous year.

HERE, however, lies the dilemma for Switzerland: In the new context of European politics and economics, and in view of its new outlook on the world, what will happen to Switzerland's proud independence, its neutrality and above all, its prosperity?

Since Switzerland owes its prosperity to free trade, a unifying relationship with world commerce would seem to be necessary. Instead of competing with the Common Market, which includes most of its immediate neighbors, the Swiss, at least in spirit, may have to integrate with it. So far Switzerland has joined the European Free Trade Association, the so-called

147

The Success of Thinking Small

"Outer Seven," an institution parallel to the Common Market but one which groups its members together without demanding any political concessions. But Switzerland's 1962 application for an associate membership in the Common Market, hedged as it was by a proviso absolving Switzerland from any form of political integration, has not yet been accepted.

Swiss economists are well aware that their country's trade dependence on European markets, its high proportion of foreign workers and its central transport and communication systems link it more intimately with the Western European nations than with any other area. They also know that the larger and more open the European market, the more secure and enduring will be their own domestic economy. But they also believe that political affiliations with other nations, such as the Common Market implies, would be a threat to their domestic freedom and to the exercise of an independent foreign policy. And whatever the solution to this dilemma may be, the Swiss also know that the Common Market will inevitably equalize Europe's widely disparate living standards and that this at least temporary "leveling down" will involve considerable sacrifices on the part of the highly prosperous Swiss.

BUT if the Swiss must make sacrifices in adjusting to new political realities, they can also offer guidelines of their own to other peoples. In 1913, on the eve of the 20th Century Armageddon, French historian Elie Halévy warned that Europe was faced with a choice between "a universal Swiss Republic and a bellicose Caesarism." Having had three decades of Caesarism, Europe at last seems to be trying to embrace the other half of Halévy's prediction by imitating the Swiss. Old enemies are attempting to forge a united Europe along the same principles of toleration and cooperation that made a single nation of Switzerland's once mutually suspicious and bellicose cantons.

Dramatist Dürrenmatt believes the trend has only begun. He says: "I'm sure if the world doesn't go to pieces in a nuclear war, it will gradually become Swisslike. We are an example of adaptation by slow, reasonable evolution without revolution. The main problem of modern Switzerland is overpopulation. A big part of our country is covered by mountains. Land cannot be expanded, but the population increases relentlessly. Switzerland is solving this problem painlessly, without revolutions or social upheavals, by increased production and tighter economic controls. So must other nations—the United States and the Soviet Union included—which will one day be overpopulated too. The world is settling down to a common denominator in which there are no longer any essential differences, only nuances."

OTHER Swiss are no longer quite so sure of the value of their land as a scale model for a future federation of nations. Swiss history, they point out, is peculiar to Switzerland, and no other country has had a history quite like it. It could hardly be expected that the Swiss example can be followed slavishly, since there is no place in the world where exactly the same conditions have prevailed. But neither can Switzerland be dismissed as obsolete, because it does carry on its affairs with unabating vitality. In an area so small that a jet plane can fly over it in a few minutes, an agglomeration of ethnic groups, languages and religions has maintained itself for seven centuries, and the traditional enemies within Europe, the French and the Germans, have come to terms there in one nation. In spite of the fact that no other place seems to be quite so ridden with contradictions, Switzerland continues to live.

The average Swiss is a plain thinker and a plain speaker who cares little for abstract ideas or poetic phrases. He thinks pragmatically about specific things. He is not likely to be known for gentleness, or spontaneous affection, or openmindedness, and any prattle about brotherly love would strike him as silly. He tolerates his neighbor because it is the one way he knows to keep his own life as orderly and unruffled as possible. For such wisdom there would appear to be great need in the world.

A Swiss train carrying German cars bound for Italy nears the Gotthard Tunnel. Next page: Traffic crowds a street in Interlaken.

AN ORDERLINESS which marks the Swiss throughout the business world . . .

149

. . . bespeaks in everyday life the reliability and efficiency that have prompted

other, more troubled nations to admire Switzerland's stable conduct of its affairs

Appendix

HISTORICAL DATES

B.C.

58 Julius Caesar conquers the Helvetii, a Celtic tribe living in areas now part of Switzerland. The country is colonized by Rome after Caesar's victory

A.D.

5th Century The Romans leave Switzerland and Germanic tribes, the Burgundians and the Alemanni, begin to invade the area

6th Century The Germanic tribes are subdued by the Franks

8th Century Switzerland becomes a part of the Holy Roman Empire of Charlemagne

814 Charlemagne dies and Switzerland is divided between Upper Burgundy and Germany

1032 The last Burgundian king dies and his nephew, Konrad II, King of Germany and the Holy Roman Emperor, inherits his title and lands

1273 Rudolf of Habsburg elected the Holy Roman Emperor. He increases the Empire's hold on Swiss territories

1291 Rudolf of Habsburg dies and the Swiss resolve to liberate themselves from feudal obligations before another emperor is elected. On August 1 the leaders of Uri, Schwyz and Unterwalden sign the Eternal Pact, in which they affirm their right to self-government. This pact marks the foundation of the Swiss Confederation

14th Century The three cantons successfully defend their liberties at the battles of Morgarten (1315), Sempach (1386) and Näfels (1388)

1332-1353 Lucerne, Zurich, Glarus and Zug and Bern join the Everlasting League, which now numbers eight cantons. No new cantons are admitted until 1481, partly because the rural cantons are afraid of being outnumbered by city cantons

15th Century The Swiss acquire various territories which later become cantons, including Thurgau and Aargau. New pacts and treaties encircle the Confederation with "associated districts"

1474-1477 The Confederacy becomes involved in wars with the Duke of Burgundy (Charles the Bold)

1476 Charles the Bold is defeated at Grandson and at Murten

1477 The Swiss come to the aid of the Duke of Lorraine at Nancy, where Charles the Bold is slain

1481 The Confederates bicker over the admission to the League of Fribourg and Solothurn. Civil war seems imminent until a hermit, Nicholas of Flue, persuades them to settle the argument by compromise rather than war. He later becomes Switzerland's patron saint

1499 Victory over Emperor Maximilian results in the Treaty of Basel which gives the Swiss a greater measure of self-rule

1501 Two more towns, Schaffhausen and Basel, are admitted to the League. In 1513 a rural canton, Appenzell, is admitted, making 13 Confederates

1512 The Swiss invade northern Italy and drive French troops out of Lombardy

1515 The French defeat the Swiss at Marignano. This date is commonly considered the beginning of neutrality as Switzerland's foreign policy

1519 Ulrich Zwingli begins a series of sermons in Zurich. This marks the beginning of the Swiss Reformation. Fighting breaks out periodically between Protestant and Catholic cantons for the next 300 years

1529 First religious "war" ends without actual fighting

1530 Swiss troops enter Geneva and drive out the House of Savoy

1531 Second religious war is started by Catholic cantons. Zwingli is killed in battle

1536 Geneva accepts Protestantism. Calvin arrives, making the city a stronghold of his belief

1648 Peace of Westphalia, which ends the Thirty Years' War, recognizes Switzerland's neutrality and independence

1653 A peasant revolt spreads through central Switzerland but it is crushed and its leaders executed

1656 War breaks out again between Catholic and Protestant cantons. Known as the First Villmergen War, the Catholics win

1685 Louis XIV of France revokes the Edict of Nantes; thousands of Huguenots seek refuge in various parts of Switzerland

1712 Second Villmergen War. The Protestants win and a peace treaty, signed at Aarau, temporarily ends the Swiss religious wars

1789 The French Revolution begins. Feeling runs high in Switzerland, especially in the French-speaking part of the country

1798 French troops enter Switzerland and occupy Bern; the ancient Confederation of 13 cantons is dissolved. For the next four years Switzerland is in a state of anarchy

1802 Napoleon intervenes and dictates the Act of Mediation, which restores the Swiss Confederation, adding six cantons

1815 Napoleon defeated. Peace negotiations in Vienna and Paris reaffirm perpetual neutrality of Switzerland and recognize integrity of its territories. Three old allies of the Confederation are made cantons, raising total to 22. Cantons work out "Federal Pact," which restores sovereignty of each canton

1815-1845 The "Restoration" period: Central government is weak. Cantons have their own laws and religious differences revive

1845 Seven Catholic cantons form a separate league called the Sonderbund

1847 The Sonderbund defies federal orders to dissolve. The ensuing "civil war" lasts 25 days and costs both sides 128 lives

1848 A strong federal Constitution is adopted, bringing greater national unity

1863 The International Red Cross is founded in Geneva

1874 The Swiss adopt a revised Constitution, giving more power to the federal Government

1914-1918 World War I. Switzerland proclaims its neutrality and states that any attempt to violate its frontiers will be repelled by armed force

1920 Switzerland becomes a member of the League of Nations

1939-1945 World War II. Swiss again remain neutral and again carry on extensive relief work for combatants

1953 Swiss join Korean armistice observer team

1960 Switzerland joins European Free-Trade Association, the "Outer 7" trade pact

1962 Switzerland applies for associate membership in the Common Market

FOR FURTHER READING

CHAPTER 1: THE LAND AND ITS PEOPLE

Bauer, Hans, *All about Switzerland, A Short Survey*. Swiss National Tourist Office, 1963.

Bonjour, Edgar, *Swiss Neutrality, Its History and Meaning*. George Allen & Unwin, Ltd., 1946.

Grueningen, John Paul von, *The Swiss in the United States*. Swiss-American Historical Society, 1940.

Herold, J. Christopher, *The Swiss without Halos*. Columbia University Press, 1948.

Shor, Jean and Franc, "Surprising Switzerland." *National Geographic Magazine*, Vol. CX, No. 4 (October 1956).

Soloveytchik, George, *Switzerland in Perspective*. Oxford University Press, 1954.

Switzerland. Viking Press Vista Books, 1961.

CHAPTER 2: HISTORY

Bainton, Roland H., *The Reformation of the Sixteenth Century*. The Beacon Press, 1952.

Bonjour, Edgar, H. S. Offler and G. R. Potter, *A Short History of Switzerland*. Oxford University Press, 1952.

Gilliard, Charles, *A History of Switzerland*. George Allen & Unwin, Ltd., 1955.

Oechsli, Wilhelm, *History of Switzerland, 1499-1914*. Cambridge University Press, 1922.

CHAPTER 3: ECONOMICS

Herold, J. Christopher, *The Swiss without Halos*. Columbia University Press, 1948.

Oechsli, Wilhelm, *History of Switzerland, 1499-1914*. Cambridge University Press, 1922.

Soloveytchik, George, *Switzerland in Perspective*. Oxford University Press, 1954.

"Switzerland." *The Economist*, Vol. CCVII, No. 6250 (June 8, 1963).

CHAPTER 4: GOVERNMENT AND POLITICS

Bauer, Hans, *All about Switzerland, A Short Survey*. Swiss National Tourist Office, 1963.

Brooks, Robert C., *Civic Training in Switzerland: A Study of Democratic Life*. University of Chicago Press, 1930.

Buell, Raymond L., ed., *Democratic Governments in Europe*. Thomas Nelson and Sons, 1935.

Codding, George A., Jr., *The Federal Government of Switzerland*. Houghton Mifflin Company, 1961.

Hughes, Christopher, *The Parliament of Switzerland*. Cassell & Company Ltd. for the Hansard Society, 1962.

Sauser-Hall, George, *The Political Institutions of Switzerland*. Swiss National Tourist Office, 1946.

Siegfried, André, *Switzerland, A Democratic Way of Life*. Jonathan Cape, 1950.

CHAPTER 5: THE NATIONAL IDENTITY

Bauer, Hans, *All about Switzerland, A Short Survey*. Swiss National Tourist Office, 1963.

Herold, J. Christopher, *The Swiss without Halos*. Columbia University Press, 1948.

Hürlimann, Martin, *Switzerland*. Viking Press, 1960.

Kubly, Herbert, *At Large*. Victor Gollancz Ltd., 1963.

Shor, Jean and Franc, "Surprising Switzerland." *National Geographic Magazine*, Vol. CX, No. 4 (October 1956).

Soloveytchik, George, *Switzerland in Perspective*. Oxford University Press, 1954.

Switzerland. Viking Press Vista Books, 1961.

CHAPTER 6: CULTURE

Appia, E., "Survey of Musical Life throughout Switzerland." *Musical America*, Vol. LXXVI, No. 5 (March 1956).

Benesch, Otto, *Art of the Renaissance in Northern Europe*. Harvard University Press, 1945.

Bithell, Jethro, *Modern German Literature, 1880-1950*. Methuen & Co., 1959.

Brereton, Geoffrey, *Short History of French Literature*. Pelican Books, 1956.

Cazamian, L., *A History of French Literature*. Oxford University Press, 1955.

Choans, Françoise, *Le Corbusier*. Braziller, 1962.

Collins, H. F., "Alberto Giacometti, Searcher and Seeker." *School Arts*, Vol. 60, Nov. 10 (October 1960).

Haftmann, Werner, *The Mind and Work of Paul Klee*. Frederick A. Praeger, 1962.

Hürlimann, Martin, ed., *Grands Hommes de la Suisse*. Editions Atlantis, Zurich, 1945.

Lange, Victor, *Modern German Literature*. Cornell University Press, 1945.

Liberman, A., "Giacometti." *Vogue*, Vol. 125, No. 1 (January 1955).

Morey, Charles R., *Mediaeval Art*. W. W. Norton & Co., 1942.

Reiss, C., "The Shocking World of Friedrich Dürrenmatt." *Esquire*, Vol. 55, No. 5 (May 1961).

Reiss, C., "The Imprisoned World of Max Frisch." *Esquire*, Vol. 58, No. 4 (October 1962).

Rickover, Hyman, *Swiss Schools and Ours*. Little, Brown, 1962.

San Lazzaro, G., *Klee, A Study of His Life and Work*. Frederick A. Praeger, 1962.

Selz, Peter, *New Images of Man*. New York Museum of Modern Art, 1959.

Switzerland: Landscape, Art, Culture and History. Swiss National Tourist Office, 1955.

Switzerland Present and Future. Yearbook of the New Helvetic Society, 1963.

CHAPTER 7: TOURISM AND SPORT

Allen, Frederick Lewis, "The First Ascent of the Matterhorn." *Life*, Vol. 23, No. 6 (August 11, 1947).

Barnes, Malcolm, ed., *The Mountain World*. Rand McNally & Co., 1961.

Fedden, Robin, *Alpine Ski Tour*. Putnam, 1956.

Green, Vivian H., *The Swiss Alps*. B. T. Batsford, Ltd., 1961.

Jones, H. Dennis, "A Sightseeing Centenary." *The Geographical Magazine*. Vol. XXXVI, No. 2 (June 1963).

Lunn, Arnold, *A Century of Mountaineering, 1857-1957*. George Allen & Unwin, Ltd., 1957.

Mann, Thomas, *The Magic Mountain*. Alfred A. Knopf, 1927.

Olsen, Jack, *The Climb up to Hell*. Harper & Row, 1962.

CHAPTER 8: FARMING AND ALPINE LIFE

Herold, J. Christopher, *The Swiss without Halos*. Columbia University Press, 1948.

Kubly, Herbert, *At Large*. Victor Gollancz Ltd., 1963.

Spyri, Johanna, *Heidi*. Macmillan, 1962.

CHAPTER 9: ESPIONAGE AND INTRIGUE

Bonjour, Edgar, H. S. Offler, and G. R. Potter, *A Short History of Switzerland*. Oxford University Press, 1952.

Dallin, David J., *Soviet Espionage*. Yale University Press, 1955.

Dulles, Allen, *The Craft of Intelligence*. Harper & Row, 1963.

Foote, Alexander, *Handbook for Spies*. Doubleday, 1949.

Kimche, Jon, *Spying for Peace, General Guisan and Swiss Neutrality*. Weidenfeld and Nicolson, 3rd edition, 1962.

Singer, Kurt, *Spy Omnibus*. T. S. Denison & Company, Inc., 1960.

Soloveytchik, George, *Switzerland in Perspective*, Oxford University Press, 1954.

CHAPTER 10: PROBLEMS AND PROMISES

Bauer, Hans, *All about Switzerland, A Short Survey*. Swiss National Tourist Office, 1963.

Bonjour, Edgar, *Swiss Neutrality, Its History and Meaning*. George Allen & Unwin, Ltd., 1946.

Grueningen, John Paul von, *The Swiss in the United States*. Swiss-American Historical Society, 1940.

Herold, J. Christopher, *The Swiss without Halos*. Columbia University Press, 1948.

Jones, H. Dennis, "A Sightseeing Centenary." *The Geographical Magazine*. Vol. XXXVI, No. 2 (June 1963).

Siegfried, André, *Switzerland, A Democratic Way of Life*. Jonathan Cape, 1950.

Soloveytchik, George, *Switzerland in Perspective*. Oxford University Press, 1954.

FAMOUS SWISS CULTURAL FIGURES AND THEIR PRINCIPAL WORKS

ARCHITECTURE AND SCULPTURE

Maderna, Carlo	1556-1629	Chief figure of early Baroque architecture in Rome. His works include the vestibule of St. Peter's, the Palazzo Mattei and the church of Sta. Susanna
Longhena, Baldassare	1598-1682	Baroque architecture. Church of Sta. Maria della Salute and the Palazzo Pesaro in Venice
Borromini, Francesco	1599-1667	Baroque architecture. Façade of the church of Sta. Agnese in Rome
Le Corbusier (Charles Edouard Jeanneret)	1887-	International leader in the development of modern architecture and city planning. His designs are seen in homes and public buildings throughout the world. Wrote: *Towards a New Architecture*
Giacometti, Alberto	1901-	Elongated and spectral sculptures in bronze: *Cat, City Square, Seven Figures and a Head*. Also paintings and drawings
Bill, Max	1908-	Abstract sculpture: *Endless Loop, Continuity, Tripartite Unity*. Also architecture, painting and industrial design

LITERATURE

Bodmer, Johann Jakob	1698-1783	Literary criticism and translations of Homer, Dante, Cervantes, Shakespeare
Haller, Albrecht von	1708-1777	Poem: "The Alps," a landmark in its sympathetic approach to peasant life and to nature. He was also a renowned scientist in the fields of medicine, anatomy and physiology
Rousseau, Jean Jacques	1712-1778	Autobiography: *Confessions*. Political and social theory: *The Social Contract, Discourse on the Origins of Inequality, Discourse on the Arts and Sciences*. Novels: *Emile, La Nouvelle Héloïse*
Wyss, Johann David	1743-1818	Novel: *The Swiss Family Robinson*
Pestalozzi, Johann Heinrich	1746-1827	Novel: *Leonard and Gertrude*. Autobiography: *Schwanengesang*. Numerous works advocating educational reforms
Staël-Holstein, Anne Louise Germaine (Necker), barronne de,	1766-1817	Critical works: *De l'Allemagne, De la littérature*. Romantic novels: *Delphine, Corinne*
Constant de Rebecque, Henri Benjamin	1767-1830	Political pamphlets, journals, letters. Semi-autobiographical novel: *Adolphe*
Vinet, Alexandre Rodolphe	1797-1847	Literary criticism
Gotthelf, Jeremias (Albert Bitzius)	1797-1854	Novels about peasant life written in simple, realistic prose: *Uli der Knecht, Uli der Pächter*
Töpffer, Rodolphe	1799-1846	Humorous stories of Swiss life: *Nouvelles Genevoises, La Bibliothèque de mon oncle*. Novel: *La Presbytère*
Burckhardt, Jakob Cristoph	1818-1897	History and art history: *The Culture of the Renaissance in Italy, The Age of Constantine the Great*
Keller, Gottfried	1819-1890	Novel: *Der Grüne Heinrich*. Stories: *People of Seldwyla, Züricher novellen*
Amiel, Henri-Frédéric	1821-1881	*Journal intime*. Philosophy, poetry, essays, criticism
Meyer, Conrad Ferdinand	1825-1898	Stories: *The Amulet, The Saint, The Monk's Wedding*. Novel: *Jürg Jenatsch*. Poetry
Spyri, Johanna	1827-1901	Popular stories of child life in Switzerland, including *Heidi*
Dunant, Jean Henri	1828-1910	Wrote *Un souvenir de Solférino*, an account of suffering in battle which helped to launch the Red Cross
Spitteler, Carl Friederich Georg	1845-1924	Epic poetry: *Olympian Springtime, Prometheus and Epimetheus, Prometheus der Dulder*. Essay: *Laughing Truths*
Ramuz, Charles Ferdinand	1878-1947	Novels: *The Reign of the Evil One, The End of All Men, Beauty on Earth, When the Mountain Fell*
Zermatten, Maurice	1910-	Novels: *The Fountain of Arethusa, La Colère de Dieu, Le Sang des Morts, Christine*. Stories, essays
Frisch, Max	1911-	Plays: *The Firebugs, Andorra*. Novels: *I'm Not Stiller, Homo Faber*
Dürrenmatt, Friedrich	1921-	Plays: *The Visit, Romulus, Es steht geschrieben, Der Blinde*. Short stories

PAINTING

Witz, Konrad	c.1395-1447	Gothic altar paintings. *The Miraculous Draught of Fishes*, with the Lake of Geneva and the Alps in the background, portrays the first actual landscape in European art
Manuel, Niklaus	1484-1530	Woodcuts and drawings. Also wrote poetry and plays
Graf, Urs	c.1485-c.1527	Woodcuts: *The Passion of Our Saviour*. Etchings and drawings
Stimmer, Tobias	1539-1584	Portraits, murals, book illustrations
Gessner, Salomon	1730-1788	Romantic landscape paintings. Also wrote idylls which he illustrated with his own etchings
Füssli, Johann Heinrich	1741-1825	Drawings and sketches, showing a flair for exaggeration and caricature
Calame, Alexandre	1810-1864	Alpine landscapes: *The Four Seasons*. Lithographs
Böcklin, Arnold	1827-1901	Romantic paintings with classical themes: *Isle of the Dead, Chase of Diana*. Mythological frescoes
Anker, Albert	1831-1910	Peasants and rustic scenes
Hodler, Ferdinand	1853-1918	Landscape and historical paintings and frescoes expressing a symbolic vision of nature
Amiet, Cuno	1868-1961	Portrait: *Woman with a Green Hat*. Murals, landscapes, still lifes

Klee, Paul	1879-1940	Fantasies noted for their color and charm: *The Black Prince, Cat and Bird, Around the Fish, The Twittering Machine*
Gubler, Max	1898-	Sunny, colorful landscapes and portraits
Erni, Hans	1909-	Numerous murals for public buildings and international exhibitions. Oils, lithographs, etchings

MUSIC

Glareanus, Henricus	1488-1563	Music theory. Wrote *Dodecachordon*, one of the most important treatises of the Renaissance period
Bloch, Ernest	1880-1959	Concerto Grosso for String Orchestra and Piano. *Schelomo,* for cello and orchestra. Choral work: *Sacred Service.* Opera: *Macbeth.* Symphonies
Ansermet, Ernest	1883-	Founder and conductor of the Orchestre de la Suisse Romande. Promotes and performs works of modern composers
Schoeck, Othmar	1886-1957	Conductor and composer of songs, orchestral and chamber music, and operas
Martin, Frank	1890-	Violin Concerto, Concerto for Seven Wind Instruments. Oratorios: *Golgotha, Le Vin Herbé.* Opera: *The Tempest*
Honegger, Arthur	1892-1955	Oratorios: *King David, Joan of Arc at the Stake.* Symphonies. Locomotive tone poem: *Pacific 231*
Beck, Conrad	1901-	Concerto for Piano, Concerto for String Quartet and Orchestra. Symphonies, chamber music
Sacher, Paul	1906-	Conductor

SCIENCE

Paracelsus, Theophrastus	c.1493-1541	Medicine, alchemy, chemistry. Wrote numerous medical works and introduced new medicinal remedies
Gesner, Konrad von	1516-1565	Medicine, biology, philology, bibliography. Wrote extensively on curative drugs and the animal kingdom. Compiled a comprehensive list of ancient authors and edited their works
Bernoulli, Jacob	1654-1705	Patriarch of a family of mathematicians. Wrote a treatise on the theory of probability. He and his brother Johann were among the originators of differential and integral calculus
Euler, Leonhard	1707-1783	Mathematics, physics, astronomy. Works on the calculus of variations, analytical mechanics, optics
Saussure, Horace Bénédict de	1740-1799	Physics and geology. Studies of the Alps
Agassiz, Jean-Louis Rodolphe	1807-1873	Zoology and geology. Studies of fossil fishes and the effect of glacial movement and deposit in transforming the earth
Kocher, Emil Theodor	1841-1917	Physiology and pathology. Work on the thyroid gland, which he was the first to excise in cases of goiter
Guillaume, Charles Edouard	1861-1938	Physics. Work on thermal expansion of metal, which led to the discovery of several alloys
Werner, Alfred	1866-1919	Chemistry. Research on the linking up of atoms in the molecule
Maillart, Robert	1872-1940	Engineering. Employed the "flat slab" method in simple but artistic bridge designs
Jung, Carl Gustav	1875-1961	Psychology. Founder of the school of analytical psychology
Hess, Walter Rudolf	1881-	Physiology. Research on regulation of the organs by certain areas of the brain
Piccard, Auguste	1884-1962	Physics. Scientific explorations of both the stratosphere and the ocean depths
Ruzicka, Leopold	1887-	Chemistry. Developed the degradation synthesis of hormones from sterols
Karrer, Paul	1889-	Chemistry. Research on vitamins, carotenoids and flavins
Piaget, Jean	1896-	Child psychology
Reichstein, Tadeus	1897-	Chemistry. Work with cortisone and other adrenal hormones
Müller, Paul Herman	1899-	Medicine. Discovered the insecticidal powers of DDT
Pauli, Wolfgang	1900-1958	Physics. Formulated the exclusion principle of atomic structure and molecules
Bloch, Felix	1905-	Physics. Developed new methods of precise nuclear magnetic measurement
Bovet, Daniel	1907-	Pharmacology. Pioneer work in developing drugs to relieve allergies and to produce prolonged narcosis in difficult surgery

Credits

The sources for the illustrations in this book are shown below. Credits for pictures from left to right are separated by commas, top to bottom by dashes.

Cover—Farrell Grehan
8, 9—Farrell Grehan
13—Drawing by Nicholas Fasciano
17 through 24—Farrell Grehan
28—Map by Rafael D. Palacios
32 through 41—Farrell Grehan
45—Map by Bill Dove
48 through 67—Farrell Grehan
68, 69—Yves Debraine
70 through 86—Farrell Grehan
93—Bernhard Moosbrugger
94—Yves Debraine, E. Boubat *Réalités*—Jerry Bauer
95—Farrell Grehan
96, 97—Farrell Grehan, Karl

Gershner—Joseph Muller-Brockmann
98—Courtesy of Diogenes Press, Zurich
99—Harry H. Baskerville Courtesy The San Francisco Museum of Art
100—Toni Frissell
102, 103—P T T Museum, Bern
107—Sigi Maurer
108, 109—Toni Frissell
110 through 116—Farrell Grehan
119—Map by Bill Dove
125 through 132—Farrell Grehan
138, 139—Photopress Zurich
140 through 151—Farrell Grehan

ACKNOWLEDGMENTS

The editors of this book are indebted to W.T.H. Jackson, Professor of Germanic Languages, Columbia University, who read and commented on the entire text; and to Fred Klein of Bern, Switzerland, and Robert Kroon of Geneva for their advice and assistance.

Index

This symbol in front of a page number indicates a photograph or painting of the subject mentioned.

Production staff for Time Incorporated

Arthur R. Murphy Jr. (Vice President and Director of Production)

Robert E. Foy, James P. Menton and Caroline Ferri

Text photocomposed under the direction of

Albert J. Dunn and Arthur J. Dunn

x

Printed by R. R. Donnelley & Sons Company, Crawfordsville, Indiana

and The Safran Printing Company, Detroit, Michigan

Bound by R. R. Donnelley & Sons Company, Crawfordsville, Indiana

Paper by The Mead Corporation, Dayton, Ohio

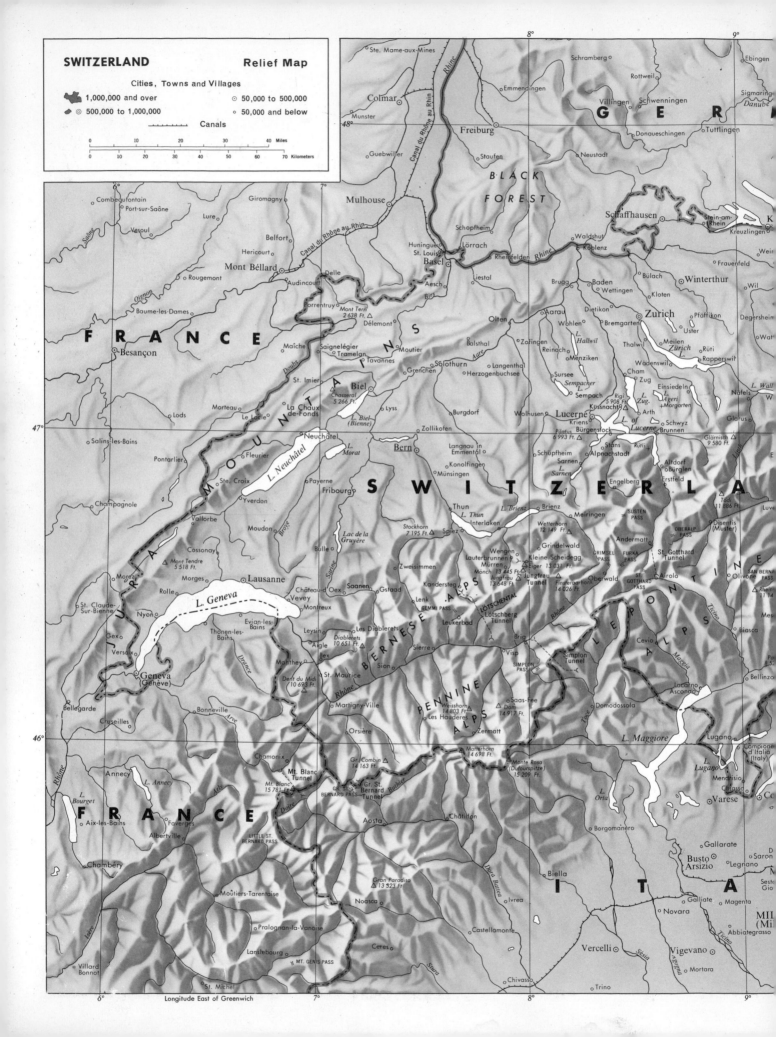